Off the Wall

Some other books by Peter Mortimer

I Married the Angel of the North (poetry)

Cool for Qat (travel)

The Last of the Hunters:
life with the fishermen of North Shields

Utter Nonsense (children's poetry)

Broke through Britain (travel)

100 Days on Holy Island

Off the Wall

The Journey of a Play

Peter Mortimer

Five Leaves Publications

www.fiveleaves.co.uk

Off the Wall
By Peter Mortimer

Published in 2007 by Five Leaves Publications,
PO Box 8786, Nottingham NG1 9AW

info@fiveleaves.co.uk

www.fiveleaves.co.uk

The play of Off the Wall
was written by Peter Mortimer
and performed by Cloud Nine Theatre Company

www.cloudninetheatre.co.uk

ISBN: 978 1 905512 15 7

Five Leaves acknowledges financial support
from Arts Council England

Photographs: Steve Chettle

Five Leaves is a member of Inpress
(www.inpressbooks.co.uk),
representing independent publishers

Printed in the UK
Typesetting and design by
Four Sheets Design and Print

Cloud Nine – The Troubadours Tour and Off the Wall
were commissioned by ARTS UK for its Writing on the
Wall project, which ran from 2001 to 2006.

Writing on the Wall was part of Hadrian's Wall Tourism
Partnership's Enrichment and Enterprise Scheme, a
five year initiative funded by One Northeast and other
partners.

More information about the project is available from
www.writingonthewall.uk.com

Contents

Introduction 7

Chapter One
Mute, Inglorious, and a Damp Time We Had of It 20

Chapter Two
The Flatlands of Solway and the Curse of Technology 29

Chapter Three
Impromptu Latin & the First Signs of Fatigue 40

Chapter Four
At Last — a Wall, and an Ambivalent Village 47

Chapter Five
Bogged Down, A Lost Flag and the Race against Rebecca 61

Chapter Six
The Day of the Bull, Hurricane Hadrian and Scattered to the Winds 78

Chapter Seven
Staying Put, Giant Chess and a Village Reception   95

Chapter Eight
TV Stars, Drama under Canvas and the Heavens
Open Again   106

Chapter Nine
Mr Chettle Under Suspicion, and Blowing the
System   119

Chapter Ten
Now we are Eight — and a Latin Welcome   129

Postscript   137

Off the Wall: the Play   139

Introduction

There's nothing unusual about walking the Roman Wall (aka Hadrian's Wall). Lots of people have done it, and despite the fact the UK is slowly becoming a nation dedicated to obesity, the number of wall walkers is growing.

It's called the Roman Wall but it's a fair bet none of the Romans ever walked its entire length (approx. 73 miles). Why should they? Defending the damned thing took up enough time effort and money.

The wall, which stretches the width of Northern England just below Scotland, and which began construction in AD122, was declared a National Trail in 2003, and this has added to the number of perambulators. It's not always an easy walk and the countryside is among the wildest in Britain. There's nothing much to do most of the time except walk and look at stone and countryside.

The first person recorded as having walked the wall was also one of the most eccentric. His name was William Hutton and he walked it at the age of 78 in 1802.

Not content with walking the wall (and writing a book about the journey into the bargain) Hutton also walked *to* the wall from his home in Birmingham, and then back again when he'd done, which gave him a total journey of not 73 but 600 miles. His writing style is a bit functional, and he would chastise people for nicking off with the wall's stone (a quite frequent activity). It was mainly thanks to him that such theft came to be frowned upon, and that the wall came to be seen as something more significant than a clump of old stone. He would also curiously record over the course of his 600 miles, facts and figures of places passed through; thus "Ormskirk, 614 houses, 2554 inhabitants." There have been other books about walking the wall, most notably Hunter Davies' *"A Walk along the Wall"* a very readable and personalised journey done in the l970s by the well-known Cumbrian author (Cumbria and Northumberland being the two counties the wall passes through).

As far as I know, the wall does not have a great literary history, in that few poets, playwrights and dramatists have been moved to embrace it in their work. I have no idea why this is, given its sense of grandeur and often lonely romanticism. W.H. Auden did write a poem called *Roman Wall Blues,* which is deliberately anti-romantic, and seen through the eyes of a somewhat disgruntled Roman soldier with such lovely lines as: *"Over the heather the wet wind blows/I've lice in my tunic and a cold in my nose."* I've never seen the poem used in the heritage industry's glossy brochures. But Roman Wall novels? I know of none. There is at least now a stage play. Mine.

Rudyard Kipling used the wall in "Puck of Pook's Hill", the poets Frances Horovitz and Roger Garfitt brought out the publications "Wall" and "Snow Light, Water Light", and it's little known that John Steinbeck mentions the wall in the story of his visit to Northumberland in October 61. There are other references by other writers, but not that many works of literature centring specifically round Hadrian's creation. The most recent include Catherine Czepkawska's radio play, "Voices from Vindolanda", a sad tale of doomed love in Roman Britain, broadcast as five fifteen minute playlets on Radio 4.

This book is the story of my own play's journey on foot between the wall's two extremities, Bowness-on-Solway in the west to Wallsend in the east. It was a journey in more than the physical sense, and was undertaken by myself, as the play's author, and six actors for Tyneside based Cloud

Nine Theatre Company. We also picked up, (and discarded) various bodies en route.

But how did the play come about? It would not have happened without Steve Chettle. Steve is the director of ARTS UK, a Tyneside-based arts agency which ran an ambitious five year Writing on the Wall project. This included authors in various different exercises related to the wall, such as workshops, school visits, commissioned works and readings. The visiting authors came not only from Northern England but some of the European countries whose soldiers originally garrisoned the wall for Rome. You might be surprised to know the extent of this historical group; Algeria, Belgium, Bulgaria, France, Germany, Greece, Holland, Hungary, Iran, Iraq, Italy, Morocco, Romania, Spain, Switzerland, European Turkey, Syria, Tunisia and Wales.

When Steve called to see me and said, "Well Pete, any ideas for Writing on the Wall?" I had no well thought-out scheme. I never do. I gave him a biscuit (ginger if I recall), paused a minute, and replied "why don't I write a play which has the wall at its centre, then we could walk it the length of the wall itself, giving performances en route."

To his credit Steve didn't blanche, (whatever blanching entails). He took a bite from the biscuit, and calmly replied, "OK, why don't we do that?"

And so we did. It took three years to organise, caused Steve Chettle and I occasionally almost to come to blows, but we ended up good friends and active creative partners. And the whole experience was, I can safely say, unique.

I'm the artistic director of Cloud Nine Theatre Productions, a small-scale but fairly flexible outfit which had existed since 1997, so we had a writer, we had a company. We needed a play, £50,000, around ten venues, and actors who could walk all day through some of the country's toughest terrain, then perform in the evening. Simple.

Though the wall itself is 73 miles, the National Trail, which we would follow, is 84 miles. What thrilled me was the unlikely nature of the whole scheme. Though I loved theatre and writing for it, my love was for the small-scale, the unlikely venue, the rough and tumble of village halls where audiences were often within body-odour closeness to the cast. Nor was I much interested in working with celebrity actors, those who'd recently opened up their houses for a *Hello!* photo-tour or were habitués of chat shows and gossip columns. I didn't want audiences mulling over the actors' latest marital breakdown, or their attempts to kick the booze. Theatrical purity was closest when an audience related to simply to the character on stage, with no baggage.

This was a hopeless ambition I knew; most actors in the 21st century measured success by the exposure of telly appearances, and writers were expected to have the same measurement. I knew actors who would sell their entire family for a five second walk-on in a sitcom, whereas there was much more fun to be had on a small scale live theatre tour.

Over the next few months Steve Chettle and I drew up our plans for the wall play. The idea seemed organic and took on energy of its own; we decided that each small venue, as well as hosting the play would be closely involved beforehand. We would ask visual artists to go into these small communities, and work with them creating an individual backdrop for each performance. Each backdrop would fit onto our specially made frame, so that every performance was unique to its venue. And after each performance the painted backdrop would stay with the community, to hang in the hall, or do with as they saw fit.

We also wanted the venues to be familiar with *Cloud Nine* prior to our visit, so we planned two more events at each venue, a theatre workshop with the play's director, Jackie Fielding, and a creative writing workshop with some of the available writers *Cloud Nine* had commissioned to write our previous plays, plus other Writing on the Wall writers.

First we had to find the venues. Steve Chettle and I spent two days working our way (by car!) along the length of the wall looking for possible performance sites roughly ten miles apart, also locations where a group of actors could spend the night. We would simply stop, knock on doors, and take it from there. A few people took us as conmen, but mostly the reception was favourable, and we even got the occasional cup of tea. By the end of the second day we had a provisional, if tentative, nine venues, village halls, pubs, community centres. Two of the pubs, *Twice Brewed* and *The Robin Hood* were very isolated. Where would the audience come from? We'd work at it.

Many of these venues were tiny, and had never previously had any artistic activity. Often it was difficult finding one person to take on administrative responsibilities for that particular venue. But over the next months we and the staff of ARTS UK got on with the job.

Nine venues, three workshops in each — that was 27 workshops to organise even before we started thinking about sorting the play itself. As if that wasn't enough we decided to further cement the sense of each performance being special to its venue by inviting the community to provide a local singer or musician to do a short set before the play itself, and we would pay the princely sum of £30 per musician.

So what this was shaping up to was something quite different. It was also becoming a bit of an administrative monster, but what the hell? I was fired up by an excess of optimism. I believed all communities bulged with potentially creative people who had simply never been given the chance to express it, so they would enthusiastically rush to these workshops.

And in some locations they *did* rush to the workshops. In some others they took a leisurely stroll. And for the odd one no-one turned up at all.

Hang on though, what about the play itself? Wasn't that a fairly important consideration? And had I the remotest idea what I would write? No, I didn't. I spent a few days cycling the length of the wall, absorbing it, and slowly the germ of an idea grew. I rarely wrote historical plays, nor am I much given to trudging round ancient monuments. I needed to find characters and a strong story with the wall as a backdrop, and thus a framework emerged. The last thing I wanted was heritage theatre. But there had to be some sense of history.

Here's what I came up with.

A husband and wife are walking the Roman Wall. He is a keen scholar of ancient Rome, she isn't. He is absorbed in the wall and has various theories as to its enigmas (of which there are several). These we see dramatised on stage. His wife is absorbed with the secret affair she has just embarked upon, which we also see dramatised on stage. As their wall walk continues historical and present-day characters slowly converge to bring a resolution to both personal and historical conflicts.

As I write the previous paragraph the play idea doesn't sound at all bad. For six months I didn't think it at all bad either and wrote two complete drafts. But self-awareness is often painfully necessary for a writer. On reading through this second draft, I felt myself going clammy with sweat at the realisation it was dross. A large part of me, the part that didn't want to see six months wasted, attempted to convince myself the play was just fine. But the small insistent voice all writers occasionally hear (or at least should do) told me otherwise. Pausing only to bang my head against a wall, I threw the whole thing away without any idea as to its replacement.

"How's it going?" asked Steve on the phone.

"It just went." I replied.

"What, all of it?"

"All of it."

"So what will you write now?" he asked.

"I'll think of something."

I was appreciative of his staying silent for the next few

seconds, and then uttering nothing more damaging than, "fine."

The play I did settle for writing took four drafts over the next nine months and was called *Off the Wall*. It was a modern satire about a ruthless entrepreneur planning to buy the wall and turn it into the world's longest theme park, encased in a plastic tunnel and travelled along by means of a mono-rail. Every mile castle is a fast food outlet, and there are interactive video screens, re-enacted battles and special chariot rides. But the theme park was merely a cover for the entrepreneur's bigger ambitions, and if you want to know what they are, read the play at the end of the book, or I may let slip a few clues later on.

And while I was writing the play, we were putting in applications for money. This funding eventually (after several hiccups) came from seven local authorities and six other organisations such as Arts Council England North East, Northern Rock Foundation and the Hadrian's Wall Tourism Partnership. We would call the group of actors the *Cloud Nine Troubadours* in homage to those medieval strolling players who would walk from village to village performing their songs and theatre, before simply moving on.

Which is how it should have been. These days for a theatre company to do a similar thing necessitated a mountain of paper work and forms, funding applications, mission statements, audited accounts and other anti-romantic aspects that can often bring the dreamer firmly down to earth. Luckily the bulk of this work was borne by ARTS UK.

I was also romantic about the journey itself. We would carry everything we needed on our backs! Simple. Yeah. Like a full lighting rig, large wicker basket full of costumes and props, the backdrop frame, the set — or maybe not.

Reality took hold. A stage manager would travel ahead in the van, set everything up one venue ahead. The actors would carry a rucksack each, containing each day's travelling requirements and a distinctive Troubadour flag.

I had a childlike desire to have these flags. I'd seen a Kurosawa film where an indelible memory was of soldiers with bright flags fluttering on poles attached to their backs. We'd be like them. I could see us now; figures in a wild landscape, our flags bravely fluttering. And it happened.

I'd spoken to several wall experts while researching the play. One thing that became clear was the tendency to get addicted to the subject matter. Once you started delving, you got the "wall bug". I also found myself fascinated both by the wall (an extraordinary engineering feat for its time), but also about the Roman Army of occupation, and the resistance from the indigenous British people. Iraq came to mind as some sort of modern counterpart, though I doubted the US (or the UK) would be in Iraq for several centuries as the Romans were here.

I decided that although the play was contemporary, I wanted one part of it set in Roman Britain, but I had to make that device dramatically watertight. It would give me the excuse to have one small scene in Latin, which could be great fun. I'd studied Latin at school, had hated it, failed Latin "O" level, but had since come to view the language with great affection, I loved to hear it spoken aloud though it doesn't happen very often on Whitley Bay seafront. I sent off one small scene to Dr Clemence Schulze of Durham University Department of Classics and back it came in Latin! And once I'd found the reason for whizzing part of the action back 18 centuries, I needed a bit of authenticity, so picked the brain of Lyndsey Alason Jones, the Director of Newcastle University Museum of Antiquities. Thus I based one character on an actual Caledonian chieftain, Briginus, gave him a wife called Cingetissa, (a legitimate Caledonian name) and included the one-time Roman governor of Britain at the time of Emperor Severus, Ulpius Maximus. Roman Wall scholars were pretty thick on the ground, they were a lively competitive lot, and not being a historically minded playwright, I had to tread carefully through history, or risk dropping a clanger.

Flags, funding, an evolving text, a list of venues, workshops. Bit by bit things fell into place. The great adventure took shape. We had t-shirts printed, mimicking those rock groups "world tour' shirts. Ours listed our nine venues on the wall, plus an extra two booked on Tyneside at the tour's end, which had come about due to the growing interest in the whole venture. Everyone wanted to see our show.

We needed six actors; not just good thespians, but also fit ones; actors who could walk ten miles then perform a high energy play. Day after day. Who were also able to gel as a team. For ten days the six actors and I would be living in one another's pockets, walking together, performing together, eating together, sleeping together (in a manner of speaking). I had little idea what psychological problems the social dynamics of the journey may throw up; neither did anyone else. When I think about it, despite the forward planning, and ARTS UK's obvious efficiency, we had little idea about lots of things. This was one reason it was so exciting.

We auditioned a wide cross-section. Some were *too* wide (in the girth), and obviously unsuited to the rigours this play's production demanded. Some were fit enough to tackle the walking no problem, but we weren't sure about the acting. There were those who were both fit and good actors, but a small doubt on their ability to become part of this close-knit team meant they weren't chosen.

I always feel sorry for actors at auditions. It's nerve-wracking stuff, and they're often made to feel they're in a cattle market. At *Cloud Nine* we give them tea and biscuits, and try to make them feel at home. Also many auditions give the actors monologues to read, which seems stupid.

Plays are 99 per cent dialogue, not monologue, and it's essential to know how one actor bounces off another actor. So at our auditions they read in pairs.

The play's Director, Jackie Fielding, and I eventually decided on a combination of the known and the new, three actors who'd previously worked with *Cloud Nine*, and three who hadn't. The roll call was (newcomers) Susie Burton, Alex Kinsey and Janine Birkett, and old lags, Dylan Mortimer (my son), Bill E. Meeks and Dave Hollingworth. We also brought on board a well-known Tyneside actor and musician Jane Holman as musical director. The play, though not a musical, would involve several numbers with instruments played live on stage. I'd write the lyrics; Jane could do the tunes and arrangements. Dylan Mortimer and Bill E. Meeks played guitar, Dave Hollingworth squeezed a mean concertina, and different people could handle percussion. Everyone could sing a bit and Janine Birkett could belt it out as good as Janis Joplin.

Auditions were held way ahead of the August production, as we needed to ensure the actors' fitness. We organised a ten week training schedule with the Milestone Fitness Centre, which was situated along the wall's length in Walbottle, to the west of Newcastle-on-Tyne. We also arranged several 10-12 mile week-end walks through the Northumbrian countryside, along the North-East coast, and up the Derwent valley. All actors agreed to participate. This was partly for bonding, partly to see if anyone collapsed, and if so, if they were worth reviving.

These walks became great social occasions and several other people joined in, including other writers and actors, and also Carol Bell from one of our main funders, the Northern Rock Foundation. Had there been any prima donnas in our acting ranks, the walks would have exposed them. There was none. Nobody came to blows, suffered a heart attack, or experienced anything more than minor irritation at anyone else's behaviour, which was pretty remarkable.

This was one of the few theatre projects to include in the budget, anoraks, walking boots and waterproof trousers (this last description was to prove a mite inaccurate). There was also an allowance for surgical spirit. Painful experience had warned me against the hazards of tackling long term walking without foot preparation, and each day of the three weeks rehearsal began with the actors and me applying liberal portions of the spirit to our feet. The pong was more like a hospital ward than a church hall, but it was a small price to pay for plates of meat slowly toughening up.

Few people in modern Britain ever walk 10 or 12 miles at a time. Many only walk only as far as to pick up the remote. There was something about this combination of walking then performing that was seductively challenging. The only theatre company I knew who did this lo-tech kind of thing was the admirable *Horse & Bamboo,* but they had a horse drawn caravan.

This book is about our journey. It is also about the wall itself, occasionally about its history. It is about the *Cloud Nine* team and sometimes about the people we met en route, and the places we stayed. It includes the things that united us and sometimes divided us. It might also be about theatre's place in 21st century Britain. Because at every venue there's some description of the play itself, and the full text is included at the end of the book.

In a fast car you could whiz from Bowness-on-Solway to Wallsend in two hours. We would be taking ten days. We would be engaging in two basic, simple, but often neglected activities, walking and gathering people together, in order to present for them a story.

In the weeks before we set off, interest grew. Workshops were taking place the width of northern England; giant backdrops were being painted at nine separate venues. I was interviewed on BBC Radio 4's PM, David Ward wrote a piece in *The Guardian*, there were various press articles in the region, and two television companies would come out and do a feature on us.

We'd sent out our own press release and it's a mark of much modern journalism that the smaller, (often free) newspapers, instead of using a press release as the starting point of a story (as traditionally was the case), would simply reproduce it in full word for word, so that in various newspapers the article was identical. Some even had the cheek to include a bye-line. This type of newspaper used fewer journalists, were less enquiry-prone, and reporters were often simply instructed to regurgitate what was plonked down in front of them. Which meant you could get away with all sorts. And people did.

The three weeks rehearsal, which included some rewrites, saw Jackie Fielding stamp a fast physical style onto the play. I was commissioned by *The Journal*, the North-East region's main morning newspaper, to write on the hoof a daily 800 words piece about the journey. It was the kind of publicity any theatre company would die for, but meant writing and filing copy from some pretty remote places. I took a lap-top, which was for me about as familiar a piece of technology as a space lab.

I was also invited by the aforesaid Professor Schultze a month prior to departure to give a talk about the whole project at Durham University's Classics Dept. These were the folk who were red-hot on the wall's history.

"But I'm not at all academic," I said over the phone.

"That's why you'll be more interesting," said the kind professor. The department members treated me gently, I met more professors than I had in 20 years, they gave me wine and food, and I consumed both in a non-academic fashion.

Our small band would be setting off into the unknown. Our back packs would carry the bare essentials for each day's travel, maps, packed lunches, water, first aid, cameras, waterproofs, and, for me, notebooks. Everything else would travel on ahead of us, and (we hoped) be waiting at the next venue, courtesy of stage manager Craig Davidson. Steve Chettle and members of the ARTS UK team would also be in evidence throughout, documenting our journey, every day it became a regular competition being the first to spot Steve on some high and remote hilltop setting up camera and tripod.

Our flags and anoraks were colour coded; I was orange, Dylan my son bright red, Susie Burton yellow, Alex Kinsey purple (well he did play the Roman Governor of Britain and purple was the colour of Imperial Rome) Bill E. Meeks grey, Janine Birkett green, Dave Hollingworth blue. What was the significance of this colour coding? Not much.

More than 20,000 fliers had been distributed along the wall's length, plus hundreds of posters. Everyone *had* to know we were coming. On Wednesday August 18, 2004, in the United Methodist Reform Church hall, Whitley Bay, the dress rehearsal for *Off the Wall* took place. It went smoothly which plunged us into pessimism, knowing the well-known theatre adage — good dress, poor first night.

I slept hardly at all that night, and I suspect the actors were the same. True professionals though they were, none of them had ever done anything like this. Who had?

Steve Chettle had suggested that somewhere en route the actors might need a day off. This showed remarkable prescience. Purely by coincidence our place of rest happened to be by far the most luxurious accommodation of the journey. We chose The George Hotel, Chollerford, a beautiful stone building whose expansive gardens sloped down to the River Tyne, and a hotel which boasted a swimming pool and saunas.

How could any of us have known at the time just how vital this break would be? Of which, more anon.

Chapter One

Mute, Inglorious, and a Damp Time We Had of It

The day on Tyneside dawned cloudy and blustery and without one redeeming feature. Nor was a damp car park in Wallsend the most romantic spot in which to start our theatrical odyssey.

We were at Segedunum, a recently excavated Roman site which at first glance looked like flat wasteland. You needed to ascend the high observation tower, look down on the site, and make use of the computerised screen to get any true sense of what the Roman settlement had once been like. The bath-houses had been renovated, and it was in these same bath-houses we'd contemplated doing our ninth and final wall performance, except the acoustics threw the words round the room like some crazed shuttlecock, so we'd settled for a room in the tower itself. That performance would be ten days distant, and we had a lot of wall to walk and lines to speak before that.

Segedunum's tower included a museum, gift shop, small cinema, and a café with the cheapest hot chocolate I'd come across. We were at journey's beginning. And also journey's end.

And considering we were setting off on an exciting journey we were all strangely quiet and reserved. Alex Kinsey muttered something about being unable to decide what to pack in his rucksack and we all mumbled something to the same effect. I'd felt stressed during packing, as if here we were, and no going back. Nerves were making us dumb.

The six actors and I would travel to Bowness in a hired mini-bus, while director Jackie Fielding and stage manager Craig Davidson would go ahead with the company van and all the gear. The idea was to arrive in Bowness early afternoon, run whatever scenes needed tweaking, then rest up before the evening performance.

What if the whole thing were no good? What if audiences hated the production, but we were condemned to keep walking and acting day after day? How would we cope? Nobody mentioned such an eventuality. I think we all believed in what we had created — but then, what did we know?

The mini-bus travelled the same journey the play would take, but with the journey both reversed, and speeded up. We passed many of our performance venues, and stopped at the remote *Twice Brewed Inn* at Steel Rigg, the wall's highest and most spectacular location. Rain descended in a grey curtain, a few wet stragglers warmed themselves at the pub's open fire and we stood waiting for the arranged photo call with a national newspaper snapper who failed to show up. We felt let down, neglected, and our spirits were hardly raised when the publican Brian Keene told us the *Twice Brewed* still had a load of unsold tickets for the performance in five nights' time.

After eating we climbed back in the mini-bus and made our glum way westwards. A few words about our cast — a varied bunch. Dave Hollingworth (who played the lead role Loot and Caledonian chieftain Briginus) was shy, retiring; Bill E. Meeks (playing Loot's side-kick Cogno, plus a Roman jailer) was high-energy, infectious, bubbly, a childlike enthusiasm. Alex Kinsey (Roman Governor of Britain and modern-day politician) had the patrician actor air of Jeremy Irons (who he resembled physically). My son Dylan (modern businessman and Caledonian tribe member) was loud and gregarious like his dad. Susie Burton (starlet, Queen Elizabeth II and bits) was petite, blonde, a look of delicacy belied by an inner toughness. Janine Birkett (Mrs Loot and Briginus's wife Cingetissa) was the most experienced actor (she'd played Billy Elliot's mum in the film), and a wise head often offering support and advice to the newer ones. These younger thespians returned the favour when it became apparent Jan was afraid of cows, and needed protection. Not that she should have been unduly alarmed. There were only about 30,000 cows along the wall's route.

The Roman Wall's most westerly sections have more or less vanished. Once you're west of Carlisle, the wall is an enigma, and an invisible enigma at that. Much of the wall here was originally built of turf (though parts were later rebuilt in stone). Its progress had little logic and has puzzled wall experts for centuries. The wall zigzagged all over the place for no apparent reason This was in direct contrast to Roman's famous ability to build in straight lines, be it walls, roads or whatever.

The reason the wall ended (or began) at Bowness was because this was the last place you could ford across the great expanse of the Solway Firth, which has England on the south side and Scotland on the north. Any further west and you'd need a boat.

The Romans did build more fortifications down the Cumbrian coastline, but hardly anyone goes looking for them anymore. There are also the remains of a spectacular high viaduct across the Solway whose main function according to some, was to allow the Scots to cross on foot for Sunday drinking in England, then stagger back, without, they hoped, falling off.

At low tide the Solway Firth, which has the rivers Eden and Irthing running into it, offers a vast ghostly expanse of sand. The road running out of Bowness, plus the surrounds are totally flat and there are warning signs about the risk of flooding. At each side of the road are deep ditches which, if you fell into, you might never get out of. This flat landscape offers a huge sky reaching to the ground through 360 degrees. It would be a nightmare for agoraphobics, and there is a sense of a place removed, detached from normal 21st century life. Walking through this terrain felt like being in a dream, so that occasionally I would pinch myself. Even now I find it difficult to convince myself the locale exists outside the imagination.

Ironically the village of Bowness-on-Solway boasts no vistas of the Solway Firth or the landscape. It is hunched in on itself, its narrow streets seeming to turn away from and offer no clue to the extraordinary surrounding terrain. As if to further emphasise its difference, it rises up on a hillock, offering the only elevation round here higher than a cow pat.

Bowness has one pub, *The King's Arms*, where landlord David Wiseman keeps a Roman Wall book for comments by those who have slogged their way here from Wallsend. Most people walk the wall east to West, the main reason being that's the way the mile castles are numbered on the maps. We were doing it the opposite way, because we wanted our glorious finish close to where we lived on Tyneside, and anyway, the prevailing wind was west to East.

The book included some choice comments. "What wall?" someone had written as if to emphasise the lack of visual evidence in the western parts. "Next time build a wall across Bermuda" a group of Americans had written. Softies. "We took a bus most of the way" someone else wrote glibly, and there were even comments in Latin, which despite my work with Professor Schultze, I was unable to translate.

Walking the wall here was, I confess, an act of faith. The only clue as there having been a wall at all was the "vallum" or ditch which follows the wall throughout its length. This vallum was often on the wall's south side which had puzzled wall academics. They'd taken it as a defence mechanism, but it was also used as a supply road.

The word vallum was first used in connection with the Roman Wall by the Venerable Bede, one of the North-East's greatest ecclesiastical scholars and historians. But Bede got it wrong. Vallum simply means wall (not ditch) in Latin. No-one has ever corrected the mistake in the ensuing centuries.

We were staying at Wallsend Guest House (sorry if this is confusing), a beautiful rambling ex-rectory and B & B in its own grounds run by Patsy and Bill Knowles. This was perfect for chilling out after the rehearsal. It had wide staircases up which often drifted the sound of classical music, logs were piled up high by the wide fire, and whole clutches of soft toys lolled about on the settees. The only thing that robbed the building of serenity that night was my wrestling with the hi-tech secrets of the lap-top, as I attempted to send over my first 800 word article for *The Journal*. Somehow the copy got through.

Hunter Davies, in the 70s, called this area "forgotten England" and not much had changed. It wasn't anywhere you'd pass through en route to anywhere else, and it took a deal of effort simply to get here at all. It was on the edge of things, on the rim, a marginalized extremity of small villages staring across the mysterious waters towards Scotland, these huge aquatic expanses which twice daily filled and emptied.

This remoteness was emphasised in the first backdrop banner which locals had produced in workshops run by the artist Gilly Walton. It was a magnificent land and seascape of vivid colours. The fort (the second largest along the wall) was a dominant feature and on its walls was painted the words "Maia — Edge of Empire." Maia was the Latin for Bowness, or should that be Bowness was the English for Maia?

The backdrops had been made separate to the frames, and the two only came together at the venues, with no guarantee one would fit the other. But this one did. So did all the others. This was some relief anyway.

Our first performance venue was Lindow Hall. Its faded red brick left it looking slightly sorry for itself, like many modern village halls where community activities have declined. Inside, Craig had set up the lighting, the backdrop, and the rows of flags which Jackie Fielding had cleverly incorporated into the action. Props were set, musical instruments, six actors' stools (the cast were on view throughout the play, and there was no backstage). Eighty seats had been put out. But who would turn up?

Eighty people, that was who. This small remote village had seen no live theatre in more than ten years, and there seemed a genuine hunger to enjoy the play. We'd arranged for this opening to the play. I'd get up, welcome everyone, and introduce the local musician or band. (In Bowness, this was The Solway Band, a folk group who wrote their own material which often featured their neighbours, so that many in the audience were also in the songs.) After the band's set, I'd say a few words, mention the specific banner and its creation, then apologise for the cast who had last been seen walking a few miles away, but were now lost.

As I was speaking, the cast dressed in anoraks, boots and other walking gear would interrupt by charging through from the back of the hall, dispatch me, and while indulging some casual (though carefully rehearsed) banter, and after a song specially written by Jane Holman, would change in full view of the audience, and get the play underway. It had to be swift, funny and energetic, and it was. At the end of the show, again in full view, and again with a carefully rehearsed casualness, they'd put back their walking gear, sing again, and stride out the premises as if the performance was but a brief interruption in the journey along the wall (which is some ways it was).

This was because we wanted not only to perform the play, but celebrate its special circumstances, though on this occasion we were cheating a bit (we hadn't yet walked a single metre of the wall!).

Like most playwrights, I expected opening nights to be

deeply satisfying occasions only to discover each time they were torture. As you write your play you drift off into pleasant thoughts of being the centre of attention as the world pours its accolades upon you. In reality you sit soaked in sweat, dry of mouth, palpitating wildly as your poor creation is dragged before the unrelenting gaze of the public; you wait in trepidation, convinced actors will forget or miscue almost every line, and when any particular line fails to elicit the expected audience response, your desire is to crawl under the seat and weep. You wish you'd taken the careers master's advice and joined the civil service. Any minor mistake or slightly delayed lighting cue looms as a total catastrophe and *hey — who the hell has left that prop on stage!*

By the play's end you are a gibbering wreck, fortified only by the certainty that you will *never ever* put yourself through all this again. You'll write novels, poems, essays, the sort of writing which people read in their own time and in their own place and not with the poor author sitting there throughout. The ritual should be banned. It's cruelty to writers, a degrading spectacle, and a totally unnecessary torture in a civilised society. Is it any wonder playwrights drop dead earlier than any other writers (a proven statistic)? They suffer too many first nights.

Having said which, in Bowness I felt strangely calm. I didn't shake. My mouth wasn't quite the Gobi desert. By the interval I realised *Off the Wall* was a slow burner in that audiences took maybe 15 minutes fully to settle into its semi-naturalistic style. Then they were away. Very little went wrong on opening night, except Dave Hollingworth and Bill E. Meeks had forgotten to touch up the Celtic tattoo felt-nibbed on Dave's back. At one crucial stage, Dave (as the Caledonian chieftain Briginus) displays it to the audience, who at Lindow Hall found themselves staring at unadorned skin. Fleetingy, I was consumed with black panic, anger, and despair, but within a few minutes such extreme emotions diluted. "It won't happen again," said Dave later. Actually it did. Once.

Generally the cast maintained the high pace, discipline and sense of movement the director had given the piece. And this one small hiccup didn't prevent eight separate people writing favourably in our comments book, including the single word "brilliant!"

The author Jim Eldridge, who writes the highly successful long-running BBC Radio 4 series, *King Street Junior,* lived in Bowness, and he'd run a writers' workshop for us. He told us he thought the production was terrific, which was good enough for us. Mel Dunscombe and her family of four came up. They'd set off walking from Wallsend with the specific aim of catching our opening night at Bowness. There were two women from Leicestershire, Karen Killins and Jess Stafford who'd covered the last 26 miles in a single day and jogged the final six to be here on time.

All this released something in us, that anticipatory pent-up tension, that fear of failure known to all creative artists. It sat, usually unspoken on our shoulders through our long physical preparation, through the three weeks of rehearsals, the grey and gloomy drive across the width of the country. But we had kept it in its proper place. We'd kept the build-up full of the kind of laughter and jokiness which all hard work needs as a travelling companion and now we felt we'd sent that tension scuttling off. This made us heady; it made us want to shout out loud. It made us forget the fact that tonight's performance was just half the story. Prior to the play we'd walked only the short distance from the B & B. In future, we'd be walking all day.

We supped two pints in The Kings Arms. We allowed a clutch of locals to tell us how good they thought it had been, and we agreed with them. We grinned stupidly at one another, and occasionally someone said, "Wow!" But the headiness slowly absorbed the fact the real test began the next day. And we wanted to be up for it. So despite the obvious temptation to slurp long and late, we walked back in a straight line to the Wallsend Guest House. Some had their own room, some doubled up. We'd arranged accommodation in a democratic rota, and on this night I got to snore in isolation.

About midnight Dylan and I walked out through the village before turning in. There was utter stillness and silence. Bowness offered that kind of silence which either put you in touch with your inner self or saw you climbing the wall (no pun intended). This was either a haven from the rat race, or a forgotten backwater where you'd stagnate. Take your pick.

As we returned to the B & B, I said, "Tomorrow we start walking Dylan", and he replied, "Dead easy man." This was OK for him — he was 40 years younger than me, and had longer legs.

You couldn't see the stars on this cloudy night. Just as well. Outside identifying The Plough, I wasn't much cop at astronomy.

Chapter Two

The Flatlands of Solway and the Curse of Technology

The insecurity most actors feel may not be that different from the insecurity most people feel. But it's easier to identify. Unlike amateur dramatics where the regular group of participants year on year enjoy the social gatherings just as much as the actual play productions (and why not?) professional actors come together for a fleetingly intense time. In this time they bond powerfully. Affairs often take place. They are part of an indissoluble team with a common objective. Once that objective is achieved, they dissolve — as quickly as snowflakes in a furnace. It is sad, but it is inevitable. And the experience can be disconcerting. It's repeated times over, so it's no wonder actors often need regular reassurance as to how good and important they are. But I'm fascinated by actors' ability to define themselves by becoming other people. This is a kind of alchemy which can turn a base reality into a more golden one. For them, and for us.

And here I was, travelling on foot with six of them for ten days.

I wished we could have stayed longer at Wallsend Guest house. Our hosts Bill & Patsy Knowles were deeply knowledgeable about Bowness and its surrounds, both past and present. They gave us a giant cooked breakfast in the large country kitchen and in their delivered copy of *The Journal* my first article about our journey had a full page spread, complete with large photograph of us on the guest house steps.

It was time to be on our way. Time to begin our great journey. The day was dry but overcast, and it was to be a gentle introduction to our cross-country trek, a flat, even countryside which in a few days time would seem a universe away. We wedged our brilliantly coloured flags on their bamboo poles into our backpacks. We were difficult not to notice. This was the idea — colour in a drab world. We had supplies of play leaflets which over the next ten days we'd push into hundred of unsuspecting hands (though most of the people would be walking the wrong way). Sometimes we would sing as we walked, or shout, or talk in small groups, or stay silent. Sometimes we would keep together as a unit or become stragglers. On one eventful day we would be scattered like chaff in the wind.

We walked into the centre of Bowness (this took 50 seconds) for an interview with Border TV. This was done at The Banks, an estuary-side location which marked the western end of the wall. This was a fact you had to take on trust, there being no visual evidence.

The TV "team" numbered a single cameraman, no reporters, and so while this individual pointed the camera, he asked one of us to fire the question at the actor in shot. The soundtrack of the question itself was later edited out. That kind of thing's become common since the union (NUJ) lost most of its clout. And the more TV companies and newspapers cut back on journalists, the more media studies students are churned out by the colleges.

Our first destination on the road was Kirkandrew-on-Eden, and Beaumont Hall. All the venues had been carefully researched by me, ARTS UK and the play's director, Jackie Fielding, so we knew more or less what to expect. Except of course we really had little idea.

No consecutive performances were more than 14 miles apart. Our universe over the next ten days existed in a different dimension to most people's. We were microcosmic. We were even nano. Every footstep from Bowness to Wallsend was linked to every other one. We were moving at a pace that was foreign to almost all of 21st century western culture, which believed that getting from A to B as speedily as possible was always the best option, so much so that millions of pounds would be spent perfecting trains and planes that shaved a few minutes off journey times. And for what?

Everything on our journey was linked to the Roman Wall — but where was it? In the small villages of the Solway Firth occasional evidence of Roman altars could be found — these were tiny affairs, and unspectacular. And there *was* the vallum, though a dip at the roadside hardly conjured the ghosts of past emperors.

We set off on this vast flat landscape. Someone once described the first distance to Port Carlisle as "a lazy mile", but ours was an energetic determined step. We were about the business that had occupied all our thoughts these last months, and we didn't intend to dawdle. We were fit. We were raring to go. The entire breadth of England awaited our performances, and we were on our way.

Port Carlisle is mainly a single strip of development looking across the Solway Firth; its heyday had been 1832 (so we'd just missed it). That year saw the construction of a canal into Carlisle itself, and the village became the gateway for shipping. The canal age was brief, and this canal lasted only 11 years before being built over by a railway, which lasted 100 years. Both the canal and the railway plundered stone from what was left of Hadrian's Wall; both seem pretty ephemeral when put alongside the 1900 years the wall had survived, or even the time it was an active defence weapon, which was more than 300 years.

Our route offered up magnificent skies and great wheeling flocks of birds, for these were fruitful feeding grounds.

This was a land of free roaming cattle and mysterious marshes that might suck you under if you wandered off. The small villages were mainly perched up on hillsides to the South of us where they could stare all day across the Firth.

Down where we walked, the dividing land between sea and land was small. Each almost seemed to belong to the other, and global warming would hardly need to draw breath to obliterate this landscape entirely.

Someone in our comments book had asked us to call into their service station at Drumburgh (but for heaven's sake don't walk into the village and speak it like it's spelt — the pronunciation is "Drumbruff"). This was the dairy and sheep farmer Sarah Hodgson. Post foot-and-mouth many farmers were looking for alternative income to prop up their precarious businesses, and Sarah's service station didn't dish out Esso and Mobil, but tea coffee and snacks to wall walkers from a kind of glorified mountain rescue hut.

From Drumburgh the road was a ribbon that stretched three and a half miles to Burgh by Sands. Despite the wall's popularity these beautiful villages seemed unspoilt, and we took a break on the grass outside The Greyhound pub for a cold drink and our packed lunches. We'd arranged for every night's venue to provide such fodder, though by journey's end we were a mite sick of cheese sandwiches.

And a small ritual was established here which we'd often repeat, as we stuck our seven brightly coloured flags in a fluttering line on the pub lawn. Passers-by would have looked for the medieval jousting contest.

Much of the land in these parts was owned by the Earl of Lonsdale, nicknamed the Yellow Earl. He'd held the title from 1880-1944. He was an eccentric in the way only English nobility can be eccentric. He painted all his cars and carriages in yellow and insisted that his servants wore yellow liveries. I have no idea why this was, nor can find any reason, but when he was appointed the first president of the Automobile Association, it's not hard to guess which colour he chose for them. The association's colour remains yellow to this day, and Susie Burton must have felt especially at home in this terrain. Hers was the yellow flag.

We flew through this first day. We felt we could walk to Saturn. It was a gentle easy terrain and we were as eager as greyhounds kept long in the traps. We walked through grasslands, muddy tracks (it was to prove the wettest August in 50 years), along roads, through woods. We followed the Roman Wall trail and emerged in late afternoon beside the swollen River Eden at Kirkandrew. Jan Birkett had brought a pedometer with her (being at the height of the pedometer craze) and every day we would take a consuming interest in miles walked, steps taken, and calories burned. On this first day we walked 11.5 miles, took 24,194 strides and used up 822 calories, which not many people did before acting in a play. Our spirits were high, and the cast seemed eager to be back up in front of its public. At that moment as we arrived in Kirkandrews-on-Eden I foresaw a totally trouble-free journey ahead!

We kept to a strict schedule. Walk one hour, rest ten minutes, walk one more hour, stop 30 minutes for lunch; walk another hour, another ten minutes rest, another hour, another ten minutes, by which time we should be close to our night's destination. The temptation, when full of energy, was to forego the early day rests, but I knew from long experience this had to be resisted. We still needed a lot of fuel in the tank at the end of each day's walking.

The day was not totally trouble-free; Jan Birkett's heel was beginning to blister and we had one broken flag pole, which needed a replacement bamboo. It was this latter kind of job we passed onto stage manager Craig Davidson, and the fact he always seemed effortlessly to come up trumps no doubt led us to take his vital talents for granted, for which we all now humbly apologise.

Kirkandrews-on-Eden was another unspoilt white-painted village, and again so quiet if you coughed in the street you'd expect someone to say "ssshhh!" from a nearby window. I was always ambivalent towards such places, wanting to escape into their serenity, be submerged by their pool of calm. But I also knew such serenity was probably an illusion. Beaumont Hall, our venue, stood in the middle of a field. A study of English village halls is overdue. They are priceless assets, and these days often neglected. One satisfaction, as our play journeyed cross-country, was knowing that each performance fed a bit of lifeblood into the halls themselves. Mrs Thatcher declared there was no such thing as society, which presumably meant little use for village halls, and this debilitating legacy was still with us.

So a village hall filled with people was more than just good box office. It was an affirmation, it was a statement on the importance of a community coming together for some kind of celebration, be it a play, a coffee morning, a bring and buy sale, or a Summer Fayre. And we were playing a small part in this, so bully for us.

Our director Jackie Fielding didn't always do things conventionally. So, although several of our hall venues had stages, the audience would often arrive to find some of the audience seats occupied same stage, with others down on the floor where the play would take place. I didn't understand at first either, but slowly came to see how the production worked much more naturally level with its audience and that a village hall stage was, for this theatre piece at least, an artificial site.

We were staying close by at the beautiful Priory Grange built in brick in 1846 directly in the line of the wall. This was not a "proper" B & B, but owners Alan and Stella Hodgson had agreed to put us all up, which was pretty brave. We arrived about 4.30, we chilled out in the bedrooms, then came down to sit round a large oval table on which everything was home-made, from the glasses of lemonade to the raspberry jam.

Priory Grange seemed straight from a Cluedo game, so that I expected at any minute Col. Mustard to descend the wide staircase guiltily clutching a candlestick. We drank tea from beautiful china cups while hens clucked in the garden. Our group made a lot of noise at such gatherings, but it was convivial good-natured noise, and much of it was laughter, and there's not a building anywhere that doesn't benefit from laughter, plus which Alan and Stella Hodgson seemed of the same inclinations.

In one of the bedrooms was an exercise bike. "In case you hadn't walked enough today," said Stella. I noticed no takers. When you ended the day, and took a rest you realised 11.5 miles was a not inconsiderable walk. And when you stood up again you realised it more.

Priory Grange had animals everywhere. There were hens and geese and the geese laid eggs big enough to incubate the baby Godzilla. I took a photo of Bill E. Meeks holding a goose egg. The egg and his head were the same size. Stella Hodgson painted these eggs as a hobby, though given their sizes, it seemed more like a fulltime job.

Our hosts were incredibly tolerant. When we arrived at a night's destination we tended to turn it into part army field hospital, part refugee camp, with bags, flags, waterproofs, boot and maps scattered everywhere, while I demanded a quiet room and access to electric sockets. And we all wanted showers, and we all wanted feeding, and we all needed to chill out, and the actors had to prepare for performance, and was there another pot of tea going by any chance? And was that all the chocolate biscuits?

I again ended up with my own single room, and wondered if the others were trying to tell me something.

Actors don't like performing on a full stomach, so each day's plan was to arrive latish afternoon, rest up for maybe an hour, be fed, then still have a good 90 minutes to prepare for the performance. Jackie would give the actors notes, which on this evening were brief.

My own problems had nothing to do with the play. I was struggling to send over my copy via the lap top. This had a keyboard the size of a postage stamp, and no idea what constituted good behaviour It was given to vaporising my words; or despatching them to somewhere in Mongolia rather than *The Journal* newspaper office in Newcastle. Actor Alex Kinsey, plus Sara Lurati of ARTS UK were both computer buffs and came to my aid. Sort of. Everyone knows a bit about computers; but no-one's an expert in the way a car mechanic is an expert, and can get under most bonnets to sort the problem. No-one could keep pace with computer technology; it ran away from us, so that we risked being enslaved rather than freed by it (was this its master plan?) and even with Alex and Sara's help, for several days the most stressful task for me was confronting the inevitable problems thrown up by small piece of shiny white technology at 6.30pm. Plus which the whole process seemed alien, as if our journey were about more simple basic things. Why did our walking and recreating stories need advanced technology? Eventually it didn't. The solution to filing my daily copy, several days down the line, was remarkably lo-tech and strangely comforting, and not a Bluetooth in sight. More of that later.

The complications this day mean that at half past seven, when I should have been introducing the play, I was hurtling out of Priory Grange, across the field and towards the hall, cursing modern technology, hoping the copy had got through, and pulling on my OFF THE WALL t-shirt. Meantime in the hall Jackie Fielding was preparing to do an impromptu introduction, and the cast were secreted away outside ready for their entrance, wondering what the hell was going on. I just made it.

"Ladies and gentlemen!" I said, trying to disguise my breathlessness, and introduced The Solway Band who once again warmed the audience up. I then gave the actors their cue to run in, they changed clothes, played instruments, joked, bantered, complimented the backdrop (created in sessions with artist Stuart Firth), and asked if anyone out there had helped make it (several proud hands were raised). The cast sang the song "Walking in the Footsteps of Hadrian's Ghost", after which came the announcement for the play proper to start. This was given by Bill E. Meeks in the character of Cogno. In a splendid pair of checked shorts, he'd walk forward, give two sharp taps on the ground with the ornate carved stick I'd brought back from Yemen, and declare loudly, "Ladies and Gentlemen, *Off the Wall* from Kirkandrews-on-Eden!" and we were off.

We were walking the Roman Wall, performing a play with the Roman Wall at its centre, performed for people who lived along the wall's length.

There were sixty people in the audience with just the odd spare chair, and I studied each one closely. As a playwright, you learn the technique of split attention. This means that simultaneously you are watching every actor's every move, but also the reactions of the audience, and if the audience does not laugh at a line written to be rib-ticklingly funny, your instinct is to stand up and lecture them on the required reaction to scintillating wit.

Some people drift in late, and your required punishment for these is horse-whipping. Similar for the woman who gets up for the toilet five minutes before the interval causing her whole row to stand. You are intolerant of anyone whose gaze or attention wanders away from the action, even for a second. Having said this, no playwright can confidently predict 100 per cent, any audience reaction to any line.

Thus there is one line in the play where Loot, the rapacious entrepreneur, dismisses the claims of the farming fraternity, (post foot-and-mouth), to be suffering economically.

"Crying into their Range Rovers," he says. Lots of our audience *were* farming stock; a few probably had Range Rovers. Their reaction to the line was ironic laughter, though had I kept in Loot's following comment, "the whingeing bastards," unwanted alienation may have occurred. And that Brechtian ambition of alienation wasn't the ambition of this play. Jackie Fielding had suggested I took that particular line out. I did so, and I realised she was right.

Our 11.5 mile walk had taken none of the production's energy away, and the audience reaction was enthusiastic. Several people again wrote in our comments book, including one which read, touchingly "Please come back each year." I was proud of the actors, proud of the split-second timing I knew the show needed, proud how easy they made it look.

Jackie Fielding had great vision as a director. Each character had a flag, (not the same flags as we walked with), which they lifted out of and dropped back into their specially made stands as the play progressed, and as the occasion demanded. These flags were used to create prison cells, burger bar uniforms, Roman spears, tunnels, Roman battalions. The production used the imagination and ingenuity to create its sets, its atmosphere, even its props, and taking characters back in time 1800 years to become other characters was made to look easy.

Later in the Drovers Arms, which, like most of the hostelries in these parts had managed to remain "unthemed', and without the blight of interior designers, we supped our rationed two pints. A bloke called Colin came to talk to us. He was putting up our overspill (as well as six actors and me, Jackie and the stage manager Craig were staying the night), and he said, "we never thought it would be that professional. Thanks."

And how was the cast? The cast thus far was in high spirits. And for us Kirkandrews-on-Eden was at that moment both the centre of, and the most important place in the entire universe, and there didn't seem many things better in that universe than walking and performing this play along the length of the Roman Wall, and getting paid for it too. So that in that pub you wanted to stop the moment and preserve it. Except you couldn't. Things moved on. We moved on. And that was how it always was.

By the time we arrived back at The Priory it was 11pm. There was an incredible peacefulness, a hushed sense of a world seemingly without rancour or anger. Bill E. Meeks, Dylan and I walked out into the garden and stared up at the light-pollution-free sky of Kirkandrews-on-Eden. It was a black velvet cloth studded with white diamonds. "Blimey" said Bill E. Meeks, and I thought how a poet couldn't have put it better.

The first step — the Troubadours prepare to set out from Bowness: (left to right) *Peter Mortimer* (author), *Dylan Mortimer, Alex Kinsey, Bill E. Meeks, Jackie Fielding* (director), *Dave Hollingworth, Janine Birkett, Susie Burton.*

Chapter Three

Impromptu Latin &
the First Signs of Fatigue

Witness the breakfast table at The Priory. Large jugs of milk, fruit juice, piled plates of bread and butter and toast. Great stonking fried breakfasts appeared for those who wanted them (Jan, Dave & Susie were vegetarians) and were gobbled down. Prior to departure we'd asked all the actors to provide us details of any special dietary requirements which we then sent ahead to our accommodation venues.

The most amusing request came from David Hollingworth who asked for a Noreen malt loaf with every packed lunch, a request that saw him occasionally saddled with the nickname Noreen. Sometimes the loaf arrived at the venue other times not. When it did we often grabbed a bit. I'd forgotten how malt loaf clagged up the teeth.

We gathered our gear together in a long line outside our overnight stay ready to be picked up by Craig in the van. This left us all with only a small rucksack apiece for the journey. The busted flag had been mended, and Jan's blister was, she said, manageable, though I've never known a manageable blister so had my doubts.

The day was breezy but dry. We were due to pass though the only urbanisation prior to reaching Tyneside. Carlisle, which we couldn't avoid, (and neither had the wall), was the capital of Cumbria, and the only town with Barrow and Kendal in the county of any significant population. Cumbria was probably England's most remote and least known county, which meant they could get away with building Sellafield on its coast without too much bother (even though they had to change the name from Windscale when the publicity got too bad), whereas proposing to build it on the Sussex coast might have been more problematic.

Most people who spend much time in Cumbria find it rather strange without quite being able to define that strangeness. To get a flavour of it, read the Cumbrian novelist John Murray whose work can't easily be defined but is — well, rather strange (and excellent).

Carlisle had a strong Roman community long before they built the wall, whose construction which took eight or ten years, depending which reference you believe. The city probably had more importance then that it does now. The present dominant castle is Norman. The best way to see any evidence of the Romans in Carlisle is to visit the Tullie House Museum which contains many of the relics found along the wall's western sections, if you like that kind of thing. You could walk round the city itself for hours without realising the wall ever existed.

Looking back now on our walk through Carlisle, and its swollen River Eden, and the flattened reeds where the river had burst through, it seems like some apocryphal warning of the terrible floods that were to hit the town the next year leaving hundreds homeless.

We stayed with the Eden through much of this day. It was the day of the pylons, which regularly strode out across the countryside in serried ranks. The river was swollen and fast-flowing enough to be disturbing, like some great powerful beast slinking past which might at any moment turn on you. In some places the river had risen up enough almost to destroy our footpath.

By the end of the day we would leave behind this western part of the wall, the section from Carlisle to Bowness which had always puzzled the wall experts. For approximately 50 odd miles east of here, the wall had been 21 feet high, built of stone with a deep fighting ditch, and commanding fantastically strategic views. The last 30 miles to the West had been built 12ft high, mainly from turf and had illogical site lines. The wall was irrational hereabouts or at least would have been had we been able to see a single damn stone of it. You could make up more or less what theory you wanted about this section because there wasn't enough knowledge to prove you wrong.

"Martian Technology and its Influence in the Construction of the West Wall" — a Paper by Professor Mortimer. Why not?

We pushed on through the city, a journey which merits few words. The city at least brought temporary relief for our leading lady Jan Birkett, and her aforementioned bovine phobia. Cows were in abundance along the wall (apart from here in the city), and we had to develop a technique for Jan to survive them without risking a mental breakdown, an all-over body rash, or whatever else the phobia might induce.

Our solution, when entering a field of cows, was to form a Roman-style phalanx round her, then gently talk her through to the gate opposite. This proved pretty successful (though I wasn't sure what the cows made of it), and little by little, Jan's phobia weakened, so that a few days later she was able to walk the full length of a field, observed throughout by cows, without the phalanx protection. Later on an incident occurred which blew this new confidence out of the water.

Jan's second problem was her ankle, which proved more than just a blister. The ankle bone was really giving her problems, and no amount of surgical spirit could have prevented this. We had in our back packs a small first aid kit, and a more extensive one travelled with the van. Sturdy lass that she was, Jan told us not to worry till we reached that night's destination when we could sort out what to do. Before we performed the play of course.

A curious incident took place soon after we'd passed through Carlisle. We were crossing a field when we encountered a young man walking the other way. He had read about the play in the newspaper, and heard there was one scene performed in Latin. Was this true? Yes it was. And would be willing to perform that scene for him? What, there and then, in the middle of the field? Yes.

So we did. Bill E. Meeks and Alex Kinsey lay down their gear, took up positions and performed the scene. Right there, in the middle of a Cumbrian field for an audience of one.

The man was called Bruno Powell, he hailed from Brixton in London, and we took his photograph with Bill and Alex. We'll probably never know if Bruno bought *The Journal* the next day to discover the same photo spread across several columns.

We pushed on. Our lunchtime stop was the beautiful Stag Inn at Low Crosby with its own twittering aviary where we encamped for 30 minutes. And our destination that day was north-east of Carlisle, Newtown Farm, Newtown, where we arrived considerably more weary than after the first's day's walking. Jan's pedometer revealed we had walked 13.1 miles, taken 26,827 steps and used up 931 calories. I amused myself with some calculations based on how much weight a person lost burning up 1000 calories: within a fortnight we would all disappear.

Newtown Farm was again clean, whitewashed, and hospitable. Our hostess was Susie Gill and family plus two Labrador puppies Ebony and Kiara. The four male actors shared one room, the two females a second, and I was again marginalized in a third. Ten minutes after arrival I looked in on the four men to find each stretched out on a bed as lifeless as a fish on a slab. It was beginning to dawn on us that this venture wasn't perhaps the doddle the first day had suggested. In three hours time these slabbed fish had to perform a fast, high energy play. Each looked like they were ready for a ten hour kip.

Which was exactly what I fancied. As against getting out the infernal lap-top and putting together an 800 word article before the performance. But a man had to do...

Steve Chettle (who was tracking us throughout) helped matters. He had taken pity on me and had bought a decent sized keyboard to plug into the lap top. Apparently a majority of lap-top users buy a second keyboard without a second thought. Imagine buying a car then expecting straight away to buy a second gearbox because the first one was naff. It happened with computers. I gritted my teeth, and feeling slightly less ham-fisted with this new keyboard, got on with it.

In the boys' room a large Victorian doll stared out from inside a glass case. This doll looked disturbing. I thought so, the room's four residents thought so too, and a quick decision was made to turn the doll's face to the wall. I can't remember if we turned it back the next day. It may be facing the wall even yet.

The sense of fatigue was slightly helped by the chill-out time, plus another large and cheery farmhouse meal round the big table. Tickets for that night had again sold well. There was again a mixture of excitement and nervousness. Bill E. Meeks talked and laughed constantly; me too, also my son Dylan. Susie Burton was quietish, and Dave Hollingworth especially so. Alex Kinsey was spasmodically chatty, while Jan Birkett was obviously worried about her ankle. Removing her walking shoes brought temporary relief, and she wanted no fuss, but we knew she would be in some pain for the performance. Next morning Dave Hollingworth would come up with an ingenious solution.

"Apparently," said Steve Chettle, "the second day's walking is always a difficult one." Despite this I was confident our actors were fit enough and professional enough to raise the game when needed. So it proved. I sensed a slight weariness in the opening scene, but then the adrenalin kicked in, they built up a momentum and after Dylan solved the problem of a broken guitar strap, the show motored through at high speed.

Every audience was different. One man when buying his programme complained loudly, "there's no synopsis of the play — why is there no synopsis?" I explained very few modern plays had a synopsis, and that this one needed none. Including a synopsis was a custom that survived mainly with Shakespeare productions.

"Well, if it's good enough for Shakespeare, why not you?" persisted the man.

The truth was many people who went to a Shakespeare play had an unspoken dread they would not understand any of it. Thus a synopsis of the play gave them some small security. Having been a theatre critic for many years in a previous life, I'd seen all Shakespeare's plays, most several times, but still understood this dread, and the quiet panic felt by many as the opening scenes unfolded (or, as it seemed, failed to unfold). Maybe not in the familiar plays such as Hamlet or Macbeth, but most people weren't familiar with most Shakespeare plays, despite what the cocooned world of drama critics thought. 99.9 per cent of the population would go through life never seeing the likes of King John or Timon of Athens. Me — I loved Shakespeare, but without the slightest inclination to stage him. He had a fair bit of support already. I'd root for new plays.

My own play was a bit less complex than Shakespeare, and not difficult to understand. I doubted it would survive as long as his works, and although I *could* dream that in 400 years time there would be regular productions staged by the world's largest theatre group, the Royal Mortimer Company, there was a fair chance it wouldn't happen.

So I said to the man, "look, if the lack of a synopsis spoils your enjoyment of the play, we'll give you back the 50p programme money afterwards."

I never saw him again.

According to our host Susie Grice, a big wedding and reception in Brampton that day had robbed us of some of our potential audience, but where would we have put them? Only the odd spare seat at the back.

The people of Newtown had produced a spectacular backdrop banner inspired by their landscape, again in workshops with artist Stuart Firth. What these backdrops did was celebrate the people's own environment and locale, which, in an age when most people made themselves unhappy wanting to be somewhere else, was pretty important.

Plus which, gathering a community together for any sort of occasion was important. Even if they didn't eventually like the play it gave them a communal experience to talk about. Many of us led increasingly isolated lives in front of one type of screen or another, and quietly we weren't very happy about it. On a personal level, I went out and met people as often as I could. It made me less lonely. And while my own messianic zeal was to ensure live theatre remained a cultural option for as many of the population as possible, maybe it was the actual coming together pf the people that was as important as the play itself. There was an assumption all small rural communities were close-knit, but in the age of second homes, long distance commuting and holiday cottages rural idyll often looked strongest when viewed from a distance.

For the first time, the opening music came from a Northumbrian piper, name of Sue Dunn. Northumbrian pipes are less world-famous than Scottish bag pipes, smaller too, and their inflation comes via "arm-power" rather than the lungs, so in theory you could sing while you played (though few did). They are hauntingly sad, raise prickles on your skin and evoke the great empty and lonely beauty that is Northumberland. One of the most famous pipers had the name Billy Pigg, which is of no relevance, but I thought you'd like to know.

That night I fell into an immediate deep sleep.

Chapter Four

At Last — a Wall, and an Ambivalent Village

A naturally evolving pattern saw certain people take on certain tasks. Alex Kinsey took responsibility for the map and our directions. Once the wall became a visible entity the route was straightforward, but in the early days, we needed a bit of navigational skill. Susie Burton, who owned the most hi-tech camera, became our photographer, and probably the only lay person to have a large photograph published in the region's leading newspaper for eight consecutive days. For which the payment of course was nothing.

Our pace-makers were Dylan Mortimer and Bill E. Meeks, who each day would set off at a cruel speed dragging us in their wake. This was to prove a mite unwise for Bill a few days down the line. Dave Hollingworth, who was probably the fittest among us, having walked ten miles every single day for the three months prior to our journey, usually chose to bring up the rear, and we felt he was our long stop checker. Jan Birkett was well versed in flora and fauna, and you could always hitch alongside her for a brief education in the ways of the hedgerows.

My job was to write the daily journal, plus which I usually kept people on their toes by forgetting something from the previous night's venue, which someone else would then spot and pick up.

If Dave was the quietest among us, and a gentle intelligent man without the slightest edge to him, he also came up trumps at the most vital times. Thus on this morning with Jan's troublesome ankle. Dave's radical suggestion was to cut away part of her boot. And it worked.

Theatre demands a lot of gear. Even in a travelling production such as this where we kept everything to a minimum, our transit van was stuffed to the roof with lights, props, sets, costume. Plus what we carried on our backs, which included our flags. I realised what these flags reminded me of when we were in motion. It was those dodgem cars at fairgrounds whose long rear poles made contact sparks that entranced us as kids. The poles often also sported small flags.

I wasn't the only one who'd slept well. The previous day's exertions had left our bodies hungry for sleep, but the gang seemed back in good spirits as we gathered for another country breakfast. Our destination this day was the village of Gilsland which was probably less than 12 miles. There was a sense of anticipation round the table; we knew we were approaching the wall's most spectacular sections. We were leaving the flatlands behind.

This was a still hot day, and after our morning meeting with stage manager Dave, director Jackie and the van we set off soon before 10am. Our timing was important. Being stressed or rushed or exhausted was no good for us at all. The cast needed to be calm, needed to approach every performance sound in mind and body. We wanted no crises. Which didn't mean we wouldn't get any.

About 120 miles north of here, countless small theatre companies would be handing out their publicity fliers to the milling throngs of culture vultures who crammed the Edinburgh streets for the annual fringe festival. We'd be handing out fliers too, but the circumstances and terrain were a mite different.

For example, within two hundred yards of setting off we

witnessed a farmer helping his cow to calve in a field. And before long this Roman wall, this legendary creation whose very existence some may have started to doubt, given the lack of tangible evidence, manifested itself at Hare Hill.

At 10ft, this example was the highest surviving piece of wall anywhere along its length, though in the 19th century it had needed a bit of bolstering to prevent collapse. Everyone who walked past it (and we were now beginning to see more wall walkers) posed for a photo alongside, but the monument didn't seem to mind. Our route took us through the picturesque village of Walton and The Centurion pub. This had once been called The Black Bull, and had probably changed its name with one eye on visitors to the wall. I'd always been told it was bad luck to change the name of a pub. It had once happened to a pub close to me in Whitley Bay and public opinion led to it being changed back. Someone had written a small poem about Walton which went: *Walton village on the wall/ Fairest village of them all.* OK, so I never claimed it was Seamus Heaney.

But hey, here *was* growing evidence of the wall. Brief glimpses of Roman turrets, then whole sections of wall themselves, becoming more regular and looking in distinct danger of joining up at some stage. And as we strode up towards the Pennines, the landscape was peeling back and becoming more dramatic, offering up its magnificent vistas. In one direction we could see the mountain peaks of the Lake District, to the north those of Scotland, to the east the arched spines of the Pennines themselves. And our route was now becoming more demanding; we were faced with long steep inclines with such appropriate names as Banks. Though the day was hot, the August wet weather had left a legacy of muddy fields through which we squelched. Just to our south (though unseen) was Lanercost Priory, an impressive edifice built almost entirely from stone nicked from the wall.

At one juncture the path diverted us off the road,

through a field, then back onto the road. There seemed no logic to it, except perhaps for a malevolent sense of humour, for the field gate bore a sign *Beware of the Bull*. There was no bull to beware of, but given what happened later, was this an omen?

Approaching Birdoswald, long stretches of wall are remarkably intact, and you begin to relate to it in a way you never do from seeing small isolated piles of stones. Stand and stare at these long stretches and you get some idea of the sheer enormity of the task of building this wall two thousand years ago. More than 25 million facing stones were used in its construction over 8-10 years, and it was garrisoned by up to 25,000 soldiers at its height. Though common belief is that the wall was a defensive measure, some academics also see it as a base from which Rome could attack the heathen lands to the north. The Roman army had advanced a good deal further than this, and built another wall, the Antonine Wall eighty miles to the north, and while this was the frontier, Hadrian's Wall became an unused curiosity. Not for long though.

Rome was unable to sustain such an advanced northern position, and Hadrian's Wall again became the furthest northern reaches of the empire. All walls built to divide nations are ultimately doomed to failure (like the wall dividing Berlin, and Israel's structure in Palestine), though being active for more than three centuries the Roman Wall was more durable than most. It was an oppressive device, yet time tempers all, and it's now looked on affectionately by the many thousands who trudge along it.

Dr Clemence Schultze of Durham University Classics Dept gave me some fascinating information about the Caledonian tribes north of the wall, and their rebellious tendencies. They often breached the wall's defences.. And just as all walls are doomed to failure, so too are all occupations of foreign lands, and for some reason, when writing the play's historical scenes I kept thinking of Rome as the USA and ancient Britain as Iraq. This may or may not suggest itself in the text.

Birdoswald is said by some to have been the site of King Arthur's final battle, which was filmed in such exquisite detail by Ridley Scott for the film *Excalibur*. Birdoswald Youth Hostel was our night's resting place, but the arrangements were slightly complicated. Original plans to stage the play at the Birdoswald site were abandoned as no space was big enough, but the accommodation was fine. Plan Two saw us book the hall at the nearby village of Gilsland for the performance. Which meant we were performing ahead of where we were staying. I didn't like this much. I felt we needed to have walked to the place where we performed. No more. No less.

Steve Chettle indulged my eccentric whims, and here was the solution. We would walk to Gilsland. The van would then bring us back to Birdoswald to sort out our accommodation, return us to Gilsland for the performance, bring us back to our accommodation later, and redeposit us back in Gilsland to start our walk the next day exactly where we had ended it the day previous. Got all that?

And that's what we did. After a Birdoswald refreshment stop, we walked the extra mile and a half into Gilsland village, picked up the van, and came back again. We felt like the grand old Duke of York.

In the past I'd always suspected youth hostels had a touch of the hair shirt philosophy, with their shared dormitories, bunk beds, no alcohol, and lights out early. Value for money, but don't expect too much fun. I'd not been in one for 30 years, so this was more of a prejudice than an informed opinion.

Now Birdoswald was probably the finest location of any fort along the Roman Wall. It stood on a high spur of land above the River Irthing with magnificent views and ruins that seemed a cut above the rest. It was once the home of 1,000 Roman soldiers, so you get some idea of its size. Not that we appreciated any of this as we trudged in, pretty knackered, stood our flags to attention along the wall, sat in the fort's courtyard, and slurped the tea and biscuits which the café provided for us free of charge, We felt like we'd finished for the day. Our limbs wanted to rest. But we still had that final mile and a half. We'd have liked to have made contact with our accommodation there and then, but youth hostel rules forbad it. No overnight sleepers were allowed in the dormitories before 5pm.

Holidaymakers stared with curiosity at our bedraggled if colourful band. We wore a variety of hats. I wore a bandana; Alex Kinsey sported an aussi style tucker hat, Dylan Mortimer a beanie, Susie Burton a floppy affair. And if people stared at us, at least it meant they were interested, so my salesmanship instincts prevailed over my tiredness, and I dragged my weary limbs along to those same holidaymakers, gave them fliers for the play and a sales pitch for that night's performance. My enthusiasm, given I wanted a hot bath, and eight hours stretched out on a bed, was slightly less than 100 per cent.

We lifted ourselves up, and trudged the final lap into Gilsland. We'd walked 11.5 miles, used up 831 calories and taken 23,450 steps.

Gilsland prevented a few problems for us. Our festive air was muted. The changed atmosphere began from the moment we walked into the village itself. In most villages we entered, people knew who we were; we'd had folk in gardens waving to us, saying they were coming to that evening's performance. Such welcomes fired us up, got us primed for the night's performance. It didn't happen in Gilsland.

There was a reaction of sorts from a few folk as we strode through the village in formation with our colourful flags fluttering but it was more on the lines of, "who the hell are you lot?"

Usually we saw a good deal of publicity for the play at each night's destination. At Gilsland we spotted only one poster, and it was sellotaped to a window at the hall itself, where Jackie and Craig were waiting. The hall looked neglected. Our performance area was on the first floor which meant Craig had to lug up all the lights sets and costumes, plus which when he arrived the hall was full of dusty accumulated clutter which seemed to have been gathering there since Armistice Day.

Another complication was ticket sales. This was Sunday, and tickets were available only through Gilsland post office. This closed at lunch-time Saturday, so for the 36 hours prior to the performance there was simply nowhere anyone could buy a ticket.

Someone at the hall said to us, "We've only sold 15 tickets," a statement further guaranteed not to send our spirits soaring. "I don't think anyone's given a live performance in this room for years," said Jackie, casting a glance round our slightly sad looking venue. But we had to give one.

All this was maybe not unconnected with the strangeness of Gilsland itself. In many ways it was an ambivalent village unsure whether it was in the north-east or the north-west. Rivers that rose round here might end up flowing east out to the North Sea or west towards the Irish Sea. Gilsland was on the cusp, and it was hidden away down in a small steep valley. Neither the main A69, nor the parallel military road — the two main arteries east-west hereabouts, touched it, and 99.9 percent of people travelling across the country would miss it.

This sense of its isolation was reinforced a little later when I sought out a large house in the village called Romanway which Hunter Davies had written about in his book, *A Walk along the Wall* and where, if I remember, he'd been given a cup of tea. Not only was Romanway a splendid large building, wrote Davies, its back garden housed 400 yards of Roman Wall.

But Romanway was a sorry looking sight. Weeds grew higher than a person; abandoned cars littered the garden which also housed a tumbledown caravan. The building itself was dilapidated, its windows filthy, its rooms seemingly full of junk. I imagined not one person in a hundred now set eyes on the stretch of wall at the rear. The whole place seemed so forbidding none of our members wanted to venture inside the gate. I did venture in, and was immediately snared in a pieced of twine which tripped me up.

"It's a sign," said Bill E. Meeks, "it means stay out." Maybe it did. But I went in anyway. Dylan, no doubt worried about his dear old dad, followed close behind. Trudging through the weeds, peering through the grimy windows at the mysterious clutter in the large rooms, seeing the general air of neglect and abandon in that choked garden, wondering about the strange caravan that might just have housed someone, made it feel like the start of a *Boys Own* adventure story. And there at the back, unseen, unloved, stretching its long spine to no consequence, was the Roman Wall's most secret stretch.

Romanway, and its condition I later learned, was a matter of some controversy in Gilsland.

For reasons that aren't apparent, nothing seemed easy in Gilsland. We dined in the attractive pub The Samson, where the food was slow in coming, and minutes were ticking away. The cast had to prepare, I had to write my 800 words, a task slightly complicated by my inadvertently leaving the lap-top one a half miles away at Birdoswald. By the time I was reunited with it and writing the first draft of the article downstairs in the hall, time was moving forward ominously. Matters worsened. The hall had no phone socket. Now my relationship with and confidence in the lap-top was precarious at the best of times, which these weren't. And my deadline was approaching.

I sought out a nearby house, threw myself on their mercy. Could they provide a "phone socket? They showed me and Sara Lurati of ARTS UK into a tiny room under the stairs piled so high with boxes and documents, and with so little room that to be there with a person of the opposite sex, you had to be practically engaged. As we tried to co-ordinate breathing patterns to maximise the two cubic centimetres of space, the door opened and a dog came in. It had bad breath. Sara was there to offset my Luddite tendencies, and one way or another, with the lap-top perched on a tiny corner of flat surface, the article was sent down the line. We hurried out into the hall and met Steve Chettle.

"You get ready to introduce the play," said Steve, "I'll double check the copy's got through all right."

Half my mind was on whether the miserly number of tickets sold would be improved by the "walk-up" when, ten minutes later Steve, who had had to drive half a mile up the hill to get a signal on his mobile, re-appeared.

"The good news is that they've got the article," he said, "the bad news is that for some reason it's yesterday's."

He saw in my eyes that sense of despair. It was 7.26pm. It was at such moments you needed both sympathy and practical help, and I got them. "Don't worry Pete," said Steve, "you get on and introduce the play, Sara and I will sort the article out."

I just knew they would. And suddenly the 15 audience grew to a slightly more respectable 40 (still our smallest), and the cast were ready for their big entrance, I noticed the wonderful backdrop made in workshops with artist Karen MacDonald, I got up, introduced the folk singer for the night Derry Yelding, who put everyone in the right mood. I got up again, spouted on, the cast came storming through to interrupt me and we were back in business!

The Gilsland performance wasn't totally without hitches. At one quiet and tender moment in the play, the local ice-cream van decided to pass outside with its chimes on 150 decibels. Later a slightly confused local wandered in through the door to create a temporary counter-attraction. These were minor hiccups.

We gave the brave 40 a good show for their money.

There were probably few other circumstances in life where a group of people, previously unconnected, would work, eat, walk and just generally exist in such intense and close proximity for ten days. We were all in unchartered waters with this production. Nor were there any precedents we could refer to. Imagine how much could have gone wrong, professionally and personally. Imagine the annoying little habits, the political and social schisms.

Imagine possible tensions in the performances, dropped cues, forgotten lines, mistimed entrances etc; imagine the potential irritations brought on by tiredness at the end of each day's walking. Imagine someone taking the last slice of toast at breakfast, or leaving scum round the edge of the sink.

The fact that none of these sabotaged the spirit of the group was the unspoken belief that what we were trying to achieve together, and what excited us about it, far transcended petty nigglings. There was also a kind of alchemy to our group, a special bonding. OK in little more than a week's time, we would all go our separate ways, and maybe some would never meet others ever again. So what? That was the future. This was now. And as any half-decent Zen Buddhist would tell you, what is most important in life is the now, a simple truth which life insurance companies did their best to distort.

There was also the unflappability of our back-up team. Steve Chettle was a natural organiser, and whatever was needed day-to-day he quietly and unfussily got. Our stage manager Craig Davidson was the kind of laid-back individual unlikely to be fazed by something as simple as say, an earthquake. We knew whatever problems each venue threw up — not enough chairs, the organiser and front door key nowhere to be found, room full of clutter — Craig would sort them. This was mid-summer so he had to black-out each performance, with some venues having thin curtains, or none at all. Electrical sockets were not always in abundance.

But that knowledge that there was an efficient team working on our behalf, and that when we got to each night's venue, there would be no hassles with the hall, was strangely comforting. In this respect we felt like cosseted bairns.

"Walking makes you feel fantastic," Jan Birkett said later, "my skin and everything feels so much healthier." I realised what it was that tired people out in modern life, and why such artificially stimulating products as *Pro-Plus* or *Red Bull* had such huge sales. It was ennui, tedium. If you had a direction, and felt what you were doing was exciting, tiredness was relative, and you could keep going. A boring job could knacker you in minutes.

But then maybe the human race *was* destined to see out its existence doing boring things it mainly hates or is uninspired by. It's just that I couldn't understand why.

I was intrigued by Susie Burton. A vegetarian, she seemed to eat very little, and had such a small lightweight frame, I wondered from where she found the energy that kept her going. Somehow she did. On stage, among other parts she played a blond gold-digger with that kind of dizzy comedy that reminded me of Marilyn Monroe in the film of Anita Loos's book, *Gentlemen Prefer Blondes*.

"Who's Anita Loos?" she asked, and I realised for her generation it was a forgotten name. Thus the fate of most writers after a life of creative struggle. Someone would eventually ask who they were. A friend of Oscar Wilde's once remarked, "Oscar, that person didn't know who I was!" "Really?" replied Oscar, "and who were you?"

Jan's ankle seemed much improved after Dave Hollingsworth's ingenuity, and the boot had not fallen apart. The surgical spirit programme meant no more foot problems in the group, and though the walking did make physical demands on us, we were up to it. Alex Kinsey had taken to much singing as we walked, and Bill E. Meeks could always be guaranteed to come in with a terrible joke. Bill had that kind of infectious enthusiasm, that childlike delight in being part of this whole programme that made it impossible not to warm not him and be uplifted by him. He was an emotionally honest person and during rehearsals had confessed to a crisis of confidence, this being his first full professional role. Everyone knew he would "find" the part of Cogno, the ambivalent side-kick to the entrepreneur Loot, and a man whose own agenda was never quite clear in the play. And find him he did, often much more than I had imagined.

For a playwright, actors' performances could bring miracles and nightmares, and over the years I'd had my share of both. Again at its best there is that alchemical quality as slowly the base metal of your play is turned into the gold of the performance, and you only hope it is not fool's gold. This depends partly on how the play is written, but also the director and actors. If their relationship is not good, is not based on trust and imagination, and the creative values of fun, the production will suffer. Some directors are known as tyrants, which I think is an egotistical waste of time, and rarely likely to produce the best results.

Jackie Fielding had worked with *Cloud Nine* on several occasions. She was a feisty single-minded woman who didn't suffer fools gladly. We had had our rows and would have more. But she commanded great loyalty from her cast who trusted her, and she brought a buzz to rehearsals, and a sense of fun too.

The further East we walked, and the nearer to home, the more likely friends and colleagues would be in the audience, so that the post-pub gathering was growing with each venue. Party time, except we couldn't party to excess. And in some ways it seemed strange to see people so familiar to us suddenly arriving in the middle of an experience that was so unfamiliar. And so sooner here than they were gone again. I also had to remind myself that most evenings, our stage manager Craig drove back to Tyneside in less than an hour. To us Tyneside and our normal way of life seemed aeons distant.

Craig had asked to walk with us one day. How was he to know it would prove the day from hell? Ignorant of the future, and after a post-show hour in The Samson pub, he drove us back to Birdoswald.

Youth hostels weren't always ascetic, not all inspired with a Baden Powell type discipline. Though people were in theory supposed not to stay up in the communal room after 11pm, and no alcohol allowed, we sat around till midnight and supped off the bottled beer which Jackie — who was staying the night — had brought for us. No-one slapped us with a wet towel or ordered us on a 5am ten mile run. The hostel was warm and comfortable, bunk beds or no bunk beds. The doors had such powerful fire-closers you needed a muscle-building course before you could open them. We stretched out, drank beer, read the Sunday newspapers, realised that, though it may be hard to believe, there was another world going on beyond the narrow confines of this wall and our own performances.

And it was rare that just the *Cloud Nine* people relaxed post-show with no-one else around. We were so enormously popular see, people wanted to with us, and why not? It was true anyway, if you'd just seen an actor (especially a good one) in a performance, there was a strange fascination in being in their presence straight afterwards. Because the good actor totally convinced you of his or her stage reality, there was an intriguing ambiguity when you met the actual person. It was unclear just what was "real" or not real? The fiction might seem more powerful than the real thing. This kind of thing can screw actors up too.

There was also some good news. Our smallish audience that night had slightly dented our confidence, and made us wonder about the venues to come, some of which were much more remote than this. Would we be playing to half-empty halls after our sell-out start? Was the production running out of steam?

Jackie informed us that every ticket at the next night's performance, at The Twice Brewed Inn, had been sold — in excess of 80. The Twice Brewed was probably the most isolated spot we would visit. Situated at Steel Rigg, the wall's highest spot, it was close to no town or even village, and the cottages around were sparsely scattered on its wild landscape. This was not an easy place to make a living. We had no idea where the 80 people would come from. Down from the hills? Out of the ground? Drop from the sky?

But the news lifted us. Also the sense of excitement that the next day the "real" Roman Wall awaited us in terrain barely altered since Roman times. There would be few flat sections in the next 25 miles. We'd be with the wall, in all its steeply rising and falling glory, inch by inch. We would be crossing the very spine of England at one of its most spectacular locales. Slowly the wall was becoming more of a reality for us, and several aspects or the play were taking on a stronger and unexpected direction even to me who wrote the blooming thing.

The three male actors, Craig and I bunked together, though there was hardly any pillow talk. The day's walking; fresh air, the play itself, and the beers left us all sleeping like babies a few minutes after lights out.

Chapter Five

Bogged Down, A Lost Flag and the Race against Rebecca

So this slow appearance of the wall proper was important. Because sometimes the wall could just seem like a load of old stones that people might tramp past in the same obligatory list-ticking way they tramped round the Parthenon or the Colloseum. Old monuments had never much interested me, nor did I rush pell-mell to the Roman Wall tourist sites such as Vindolanda or Housesteads.

But Birdoswald seemed different from the moment you walked out onto the elevated site. It was as if it lifted you entirely and took you back 1900 years. You didn't need an actor dressed as a centurion, an info video, a brochure, a souvenir shop or anything like that. You needed simply to stand here among these tall pillars sprouting from the ruins, hear the wind in the high trees, absorb the spectacular views of wild and beautiful countryside the site offered. There was little evidence of modernity, and hardly any visitors this early in the morning. What you saw was either Roman or simply the natural unspoilt world.

As well as the ruins, the Birdoswald site overall impressed, with its courtyard, its attractive stone buildings, the small shop and café, its idiosyncrasies such as workshops where you could make a Roman helmet. But also the sense it had created its own world, it was a quiet celebration of the past without either cheapening it or preserving it in aspic. There wasn't a great deal to see in the Birdoswald ruins. But there was a lot to feel.

Having our director Jackie stay overnight spoiled us. First, the free beer the night before, now at breakfast she set to in the bright and gleaming kitchen making bacon and eggs for the whole crew (veggies apart). I gobbled down the grub with gusto (too much alliteration author...). It was part of the simple Mortimer diet. Eat heartily. Then use it up. All the rest was propaganda.

We had been on the road four days, and thus far I'd found it impossible to take a shower. Our venues were usually ill-suited to housing seven or eight people. Shower facilities were often minimal (one per venue). No sooner did we arrive late afternoon than I was forced to grapple with the lap-top and my overnight article. By the time this was done, and we had eaten, it was usually time for the show to go up. And in the mornings people were queuing up for the shower, and I was left with the sink.

When I confessed this ablutions omission to the rest they were aghast, and backed away as if to suggest I was contagious. Explaining I'd had several all-over washes in this time did not impress them .To stay showerless for four days in modern Britain was simply not on. But here was my chance. Birdoswald had showers in abundance so I took two in quick succession, emerging pink and sweet-smelling for the exertions of the day. Because this was to be in the serious part of wall walking. With our bright flags fluttering like trapped bird wings, we would be a Technicolor ribbon snaking its way across an increasingly spectacular landscape.

And it was only when our well-oiled and efficient machine went wrong that we noticed it at all. Thus this morning, a glitch meant no packed lunches had been prepared. The Samson pub, where the previous evening we'd waited a long time for fodder, came to our aid, and offered to make lunches up at short notice. Not short enough though for us to delay our obligatory 10am start. This starting time was a point of honour for me; to risk missing it brought out all my sergeant-major authoritarian side, character traits I would scoff at in others. So the packed lunches could catch us up later, courtesy of Jackie and Craig, who would be tracking us through the day.

The van ferried us into Gilsland, the exact spot centre village we had finished walking the day previously. Gilsland still had the air of the forgotten village, crouching down to hide from the world proper. I was unsure if I found it attractive or unnatural, and was still pondering when we struck out.

We were coming into Whin Sill country. This was the wall's highest, most spectacular and most isolated section but ironically the one most visited, because humans sometimes needed to get away from their fellow humans, whose company mainly they craved.

Not that you'd jostle people here like you might on Blackpool sea front. Crowded was a relative term. Plus which most wall walkers were quiet, unobtrusive, and rarely wore *Kiss me Quick* hats, so a few hundred of them didn't seem that many, especially when plonked down in these vast spaces.

Our day was a staggering dragon's back of a journey, an energy-draining but breathtaking experience as the wall plunged and soared with the kind of curves to make a big dipper green with envy.

In these parts the wall is an impossible construction. Who would ever construct at these angles, and almost 2000 years ago? What mad desire for empire-building spurred the Romans on? Wouldn't it have been easy just to stay round Colchester and have the easy life?

Again I felt that ambivalence towards empires, the distaste for the desire to conquer and subjugate other peoples coupled with a sneaking admiration for the energy and imagination needed to do it. It had happened from a fairly small base, both with Rome, and later with Britain. Both empires crumbled as all empires must, both were ruthless and often cruel, but also extraordinary. And when writing the play, and specially the scenes in Roman Britain, I felt that ambivalence always at my shoulder.

Our view to the North this day was a landscape virtually unaltered since the Romans laid the first stone. During the day we would traverse crags with sides as sheer as sliced cake. We would suffer the most extreme weather thus far and for the first time we would need to pull on our waterproofs. As we battled in the teeth of high winds and rain we would look more like a band of Sherpas than a theatre company, and as the elements and terrain grew more extreme, so too would our emotions.

The early part of the day was marked by two incidents. First my precious flag went missing. This happened somewhere near the ruins of Thirwall castle, built in stone plundered from the wall by John Thirwall in 1330. The castle was said to contain a golden table hidden down a well. I'd have settled for my flag. The ruins were officially described as "melancholic" and I felt melancholic too. My orange flag was part of my identity, it defined me, and it marked me out as part of this great adventure and not just another wall walker. And now it had gone, somehow come loose from my backpack without anyone noticing. I felt like Zorro without his sword, Otto Klemperer without his conductor's baton. The flag lay somewhere on a roadside, or on a muddy track. I ran back over our last mile, but there was no sign of it. The next five days without my trusty flag? Unthinkable. For the rest of that day, every single walker heading in the direction we had come, was briefed on the missing flag, and given a contact number should they find it.

Now let me say not everyone in the party shared my flag obsession. There were times on the journey when actors removed their flags and used them as walking sticks, which made me bite my sergeant-major lip in frustration, and even as I railed against my loss this morning, circumstances meant the "bereavement" did not always elicit huge sympathy.

Let me explain. Craig turned up with the packed lunches. He pulled the van onto the roadside and it immediately sank to its axles in a cunningly disguised boggy stretch of grass. He was stuck. Meantime, Steve Chettle and Sara had positioned themselves up on a distant and totally exposed hilltop with a tripod to take pictures of us snaking our way up the hillside. The lost flag had already delayed us. The sunken vehicle delayed us more, so that over the next 90 minutes, while Steve futilely scanned the hill for sign of flag-bearing humans, he and his assistant Sara slowly crystallised into ice. And down in the valley we were staring at our sunken van on this tiny, little-used country road, while ahead the Roman Wall raced away, as if mocking us.

Not the best start to a day. The creaking I could hear was the cast's good nature straining. I was still quizzing people as to how they could not have spotted the flag drop from my backpack. We had two people freezing on a hill top, we had a van with all the gear sinking into oblivion, our schedule was running increasingly late, so it was perhaps excusable that I heard a whispered voice behind me say, "bugger the flag" even if the words left me far too upset to turn round and identify the speaker.

The joys of travelling theatre! But the fates took *some* pity on us, and two guardian angels came to the van's aid in the shape of Pete Moorhead and Keith Weeks of Northumberland National Park, who were out repairing gates. Their Land Rover winched our poor van from its swampy confinement. Did they realise they had saved that evening's performance? No. Would they take anything for their efforts? No thanks. Would they like to come and see the show with our compliments? Doubtful.

A third incident too, a little earlier. We were climbing the steep side of Greenhead Hill when BBC Radio Newcastle rang one of our mobiles to do a live on-air interview.

This was one of the more peculiar media interviews I'd ever done. There were obligatory questions about our progress, the play, audiences, mishaps, after which the interviewer paused and said, "You sound very much out of breath, it must be very hard going out there."

"It is at the moment," I replied, "I'm staggering up a one in four gradient." Never once did I think of stopping.

Nor was this the only interview peculiarity. A certain Nancy Rodham was relaxing in her kitchen, listening to the radio. There was this breathless playwright talking about walking a play the length of the Roman Wall. He mentioned Greenhead Hill, which was directly in line with her kitchen window. She looked out and there was the playwright, in transit, and being interviewed live on air.

The detectives among you may wonder how I knew this. Because when we finally arrived at Twice Brewed, Nancy Rodham was perched on a bar stool, and she told me all about it.

Post-Thirwall Castle we were on high terrain. We were figures in a landscape; we were dwarfed both by nature and by the sheer impudence of this crazy wall which leapt its high hurdles just as effortlessly as a Grand National steeple-chaser. The landscape also dwarfed our petty differences.

The weather was worsening and the forecast had clearly discouraged all but the hardiest of wall walkers. We did see one unlikely couple several times this day. It was Andrew Hartley of Sheffield and his resilient eight year old daughter Rebecca. Rebecca was desperate to see our play, but had heard all tickets were gone. She had convinced herself that if she and her father arrived at Twice Brewed before the actors, they'd be guaranteed a seat. We told her dad we'd fix it to ensure they'd both get in, but Rebecca was taking no chances. Every time we stopped for a short break, Rebecca came hurtling past us with a look of sheer fortitude on her face. We'd walk past her a little later. But come the next stop, we'd be watching out for the hurtling Rebecca and she didn't let us down. And who got to Twice Brewed first, despite the terrible conditions? Rebecca.

We stopped for lunch that day in a sheltered wood clearing, and hardly had we munched on the cheese sandwiches than the first drops of rain plopped onto the beef flavoured crisps. Nor was this a quick shower. The rain would be incessant for the rest of the day's journey. We gathered up our bits, put on our waterproofs and struck out.

Rain silences you, reduces you to hunched figures strung out along the wall. It wasn't long before our waterproofs proved themselves in default of the trades description act, and welcomed in the water, so that an uncomfortable dampness began to seep into our clothing. We passed several quarries below us. To take my mind off the weather I mused over the fact most people thought these quarries had been mined by the Romans to build the wall. Not so. Generally the Romans found the whinstone too hard to deal with, and settled for sandstone. Where they got all the sandstone from has never been properly resolved. The quarries were mined several centuries later.

I knew that eventually along this high exposed sill, we would spot below in the distance the distinctive whitewashed building of the Twice Brewed pub and hotel. It couldn't come soon enough.

The weather had dampened our spirits, I was still sulking over the lost flag, and the terrain was hard going, so the eventual sighting of Twice Brewed was a welcome antidote. We'd passed the wall's highest point on this day's walk, the redundant OS trig point on Windshields Crags where Dylan, showing the well-known Mortimer penchant for exhibitionism, stood on top with arms outstretched like that Rio de Janeiro Christ sculpture.

The trig point is 1132 feet above sea level, so global warming floods should pose no threat. And from hereabouts you get one of the wall's most famous views, though they come thick and fast on this day. Crag Lough lies far below, and like all the water we pass on this day, it is both spectacular and disturbing, as if somehow it did not belong up here in these exposed windy heights, as if these small lakes had been transplanted and held some dark secret. What added to the sense of the disturbance was the fact the lakes had no natural shoreline; the water dissipated into marshy reeds where you would not wish to wander.

And with long continuous stretches of wall, you began to understand the Roman system. The Roman mile castle did exactly what it said on the tin. Roman miles were slightly shorter than our own, but whatever the location when one mile was up, the mile castle was built, no matter if the terrain were difficult or steeply sloping. Mile castles could originally offer accommodation for up to four soldiers, and there were probably still the remains of enough of them to make a whizzkid marketeer from the likes of Holiday Inn sit up and think of redevelopment — which was straying into the area of my play. Between the mile castles were usually a couple of turrets, two storey observation towers, and you could come across the occasional fort, of which more later.

You might be intrigued by the name The Twice Brewed, especially as right next to it is a youth hostel called The Once Brewed. I'll tell you the generally accepted reason behind the names later, and also why the present landlord thinks the conventional explanation is a load of baloney.

It's also a good time to tell you a little more about William Hutton, the first man to walk the Roman Wall in 1802. He stayed the night at The Twice Brewed, and there's a rather jovial oil painting by an artist called Ronald Embleton which captures the occasion. Nine cheerful if somewhat greedy looking gentlemen are tucking into their vittals round a large wooden table inside the inn. In the background is a roaring fire. The landlord (I assume it is he) is standing with a large metal jug of ale ready to replenish their beer glasses. Also in the background is Hutton himself, knees together, sitting somewhat decorously and in his hand is what looks like a glass of wine.

Hutton seems the outsider who would like to be invited in, but hasn't been. I identified immediately with the painting, having spent a winter on Holy Island and for several Wednesday nights, I was stood at one end of the only bar open midweek on the island. At the other end, the only other customers, a group of local men engaged in conversation from which I knew was excluded.

Hutton's *History of the Roman Wall* was published in 1813, republished by Frank Graham in Newcastle in 1990 but is now difficult to track down. Hutton walked the wall east to west, like most of his successors, and regularly refers not to Hadrian's Wall but Severus' Wall. There's a case to be made for this as Emperor Severus was equally as, if not more responsible than Emperor Hadrian for the wall's construction, and/or its refortification after the failure of the Antonine Wall 80 miles north. Hadrian paid only one visit to Britain, and was in fact a Spaniard. Come to that Severus was Libyan.

Hutton could be very impolite. On walking through Penrith he concluded, "a more dreary country than this can scarcely be conceived". But it was down to him that people began to take seriously the wall's preservation, and it was only after his book that nicking off with the wall's stone was viewed with any kind of disapproval. The book's modern edition front cover shows Hutton trying to stop the dismantling of the wall at Planetrees (which we would eventually pass), and there's also a mention of him despatching a servant to chastise a certain Henry Tulip for stealing stone from the wall to build a farmhouse at the site of St. Oswalds.

Hutton is undeservedly forgotten in English literary history. On his journey his daughter Catherine would ride ahead of him on horseback, fix up his accommodation and handle his money. In this, she was a bit like our stage manager Craig Davidson.

A final word about Hutton. He wrote 13 books in total, including *A History of Blackpool*, a title which alone deserves to ensure literary immortality. In fact all his books have passed into obscurity. I have a soft spot for him. Like me he took notes as he went along, and also like me he would often make mistakes when referring to these notes, on one occasion confessing he had totally forgotten the name of the person he was writing about. Good old William Hutton.

From first spotting the Twice Brewed to arriving was maybe an hour's walking, the final part dropping down from the high crags onto a tarmac road (one of the few roads to bisect the wall). This road descended and eventually met up with the Military Road. The latter had a bizarre history (more of which later). A quarter of a mile along the Military Road was the Twice Brewed. There was enormous relief to have arrived, so much so that as we walked those final yards, wet, bedraggled, and tired, we spontaneously broke out into the Snow White song "Hi Ho! Hi Ho!" (well, there were seven of us), somewhat to the amazement of the few folk gathered in the pub doorway to greet us.

Singing unites the world, and it united us, so that by the time we sat with a huge pot of tea in the pub's bar the differences of the day had fallen away. Plus which I had especially looked forward to Twice Brewed. I'd visited this remote setting several times since the wall play idea took hold. I had even given a poetry reading here one Saturday night as part of the whole *Writing on the Wall* project. It had been a bizarre occasion, reading nonsense poetry to people as they tackled their peppered steaks and *sole meuniere*. Many of the diners had not been expecting it, and stared hard at their dinner plates, unsure what to make of their weekend gourmet treat being accompanied by the likes of Gladys the Tadpole and Bald Bertie. Not that you could let such things deter you.

The Twice Brewed had one long bar more or less the length of the building's frontage. Behind was a restaurant which we'd converted for the night's performance. There were enough bedrooms to accommodate our team plus various other people who were travelling out specially to see the show.

We arrived at 4pm and as we drank the tea, we checked the pedometer. This revealed a journey of 10.5 miles (all hard won), 20,966 steps taken, and 745 calories used up. I wanted us one day to break the 1000 calorie marker — that's like making an entire Big Mac disappear which can't be a bad thing.

All the bedrooms looked out across the Military Road, then up the steep hillside to where at the distant summit the wall spectacularly rode along the bucking bronco that was Steel Rigg, or at least would have done had not a thick fog descended blotting out everything more than 25 yards distant.

Each night our sleeping combinations were different. Here I was doubling up with my son Dylan who, before the night was out, would be locking himself in that same room covered in shame

The landlord Brian Keen was a canny Scouser and this was a highly individual pub. Remote it may have been but it boasted its own internet café (no need of the cursed lap top to send that night's article!), was the only place I knew that sold poteen coffee, and had three cask bitters called Flavius, Summis and Fortis, which sounds like a firm of Roman solicitors.

There were a few sore feet at the end of this day, but nothing serious. Jan Birkett's cut-away boot had done its job, though she was looking somewhat peaky as we sat round the large bar table. "I'm just feeling a bit sick," she said, "I'll go and lie down." That seemed to do the trick, and by show time she was back on top form.

There was glue that united us. The glue was the next performance. Actors are often insecure, but have a steely determination when it comes to getting out on that stage, so that I knew every step we took along the wall was fortified by this determination, this desire to get up in front of a live audience and create that alchemic mix that came from the combined talents of writing, directing, and acting. A play was a nebulous ephemeral affair. Though it could exist on the page (and does so in this book) any one performance was by definition transitory and impossible to reproduce. This was both sad but part of the attraction, the knowledge that at that moment in that location you had to do it to the best possible way, because that particular occasion would never arise again. Just like life really. And Twice Brewed would create some unforgettable moments, though one at least, the actor would no doubt sooner forget as soon as possible.

A huge surprise awaited me. How was I to know that during this day's walking, which had been occasionally short-tempered and frustrating, Craig and Jackie had made great efforts to find my flag, Steve Chettle and Sara Lurati had also made great efforts to find my flag, and that these efforts had paid off, and my flag had been found earlier in the day, but Jackie had asked everyone to say nothing so that there could be an unexpected event once we arrived at Twice Brewed.

And there in the bar stood young Oscar Cass-Darweish of Birmingham (had he walked from that city like William Hutton?) and he was holding my wonderful orange flag which had had spotted by the side of a road, and somehow the Cloud Nine gang had engineered to have him present me with right there. Oscar was my all-time great hero. Come to that, so were the rest of them, and me thinking they couldn't give a tinker's cuss about my flag.

Everything went right at Twice Brewed. The returned flag, the sell-out audience, and the internet café enabling the most trouble-free experience thus far in getting my article over to *The Journal*.

And the performance was unlike anything we'd experienced so far. Jackie and Craig had decided to do the show broadsides on which produced fewer rows of seats, but much wider rows. Two problems presented themselves. There was a low ceiling which meant our fancy flag routines needed to be modified. The flags had to be taped to indicate to the actors exactly where they were to hold them if we weren't to stab holes in that same ceiling. And the performance floor was carpeted which would reduce greatly the dramatic staccato effect we often achieved banging these flags down. The cast had to strike particularly hard, but even so the effect was muted.

All eighty tickets had been sold but it was clear there were still a good many people wanting to get in. Both Jackie and I were loathe to turn people away, especially at such an isolated venue as Twice Brewed. It wasn't as if audiences would just have walked up the street to be here, or have hopped on a 28 bus. Everyone who'd come to see this performance had made a special effort. Among those without tickets was a group of Americans from New Jersey who were walking the wall attempting to raise 10,000 dollars for leukaemia research. Jackie came up with a brilliant idea. Because the show was sold out, and our budget income line had been achieved here, she suggested we found room for the Americans, and they could contribute the ticket money towards their fund. This boosted it by some £45.

Somehow we found places for everyone. More than one hundred people eventually crammed into that back room, in that isolated pub. Outside a thick mist had descended blotting out the Roman wall completely. It was an inhospitable a night in as exposed a setting as you could imagine, yet the whole evening pulsated. As more people arrived we said, "If you can find a seat, you can come in." This led to the public bar being raided for chairs and stools, till soon it was pretty empty of furniture, but as virtually everyone in the building was there to see the play, no matter. And yes, we did find a place for young Rebecca Hartley and dad Andrew, and I think if Desperate Dan had turned up we'd have found a place for him too.

And despite the crush we had to keep gangways clear, firstly for the actors to make their entrance, but also for fire regulations, so that we were pushing and squashing and re-arranging everyone, and the whole place was heaving. There was another eye-catching backdrop, made in workshops with artist Karen McDougall, and to start the evening there was the veteran Bardon Mill concertina player Henry Robson with a string of well-known rousing North-East songs, which an exuberant and seemingly totally uninhibited audience sang along to unbidden. Henry ended with the North-East's unofficial anthem *The Blaydon Races*, which everyone in the region knows *some* of the words to even though there are nine million verses. By this time, with the play not even yet started, the rafters were being lifted, though admittedly same rafters were pretty low to start with.

We had lots of acquaintances in that night too, family, friends, plus some fellow actors from NTC Touring Company based in Alnwick, who'd kindly lent us their lighting rig for the tour (our own being a bit minimal). Actors always want to turn it on for their fellow professionals, though our cast needed no psyching up. In fact when they ran out through the narrow audience channel we'd kept open for them, it was like they'd been fired from a gun.

Is this a good moment to think about that name, Twice Brewed? The common belief is that the unusual moniker is down to General Wade who built this military road in the 18th century following the advance to Carlisle of Bonnie Prince Charlie. The English were unable to despatch their forces quick enough across the country to stop Chuck's ambitions, and to prevent any re-occurrence in 1745 Wade proposed that a brand new linking road, 27 miles long should be built and that the Roman Wall should be used as the bedrock. The road was actually authorised in 1751 by which time Wade was dead. So that often along this stretch of the journey, if you are unable to spot the Roman Wall, it's because you're walking on top of it. Pillaging the ancient monument in this way has been described as "the greatest act of vandalism in the history of Britain," though given some of the antics we've got up to over the centuries, this might be slightly hyperbolic.

Wade was said to have stopped at the inn, taken a sup of the local beer and complained that it was too weak. Off they went and brewed it again, more to his satisfaction, and thus the name was born. Presumably, the youth hostel next-door (The Once Brewed) was not involved. It is an attractive yarn, even if a similar complaint in most of the UK hostelries about beer today would be unlikely to result in such a satisfactory response. Twice Brewed landlord Brian Keen describes the tale as tosh.

"For a start," he says, "the building wasn't even here at the time, and as General Wade was dead, how could he have come here anyway?" Brian claims the name derives from the words two brewes, or hills, and certainly there are plenty of them hereabouts. A writer with a more academic bent than I would at this point be scurrying off to discover the true facts about Twice Brewed, but I quite like the ambiguity, and we had a show to put on.

There was something almost spontaneously combustible about the audience at Twice Brewed. At each performance I stood at the rear, ready for the play to do its job slowly at first, so that for the opening ten minutes or so, the audience, most of whom would not have seen much modern live theatre, would be growing used to the style. As our tour progressed, this bothered me less and less, and I came to enjoy the metamorphosis, the change in atmosphere, that gradual coming together of play and audience. Once the two were united, we were really motoring.

But at Twice Brewed there was an immediate reaction. Maybe it was the sense of anticipation of the tightly packed audience out here at this isolated spot with the wild fog-bound hills just beyond those four walls. Maybe it was because the audience was more than usually sprinkled with friends and fellow theatre people. Whatever, from the opening lines of the play, as the ruthless entrepreneur Loot (Dave Hollingworth) simultaneously rewards and degrades the small businessman Drysdale (Dylan Mortimer), whose business he is taking over, the response was fast and enthusiastic.

And actors feed off such response. They become ten foot tall. They become immortal. So that here at the highest point of the Roman Wall, all six acted out of their skins.

And you wanted to bottle the experience, preserve it to be savoured again at a later date. Not possible.

The performance (and probably the headiness of the occasion) produced one of the tour's strangest moments. Every actor knows the technique when occasionally the next word in the script eludes them, and they need that nano-second to find it, so that some "stopgap" word is used to fill the pause.

In the later stages of the play, Dylan, playing a Caledonian tribesman captured by the Romans at Vindolanda says the line, "The Caledonians won't rest till we've kicked every Roman out of Britain." It is a line supposed to be issued with emotion, but on this night the emotion went too far, and in front of the word "Caledonian" Dylan inserted the word "fucking".

It is only two syllables, and it is a word which the last two decades has been divested of much of its ability to shock. Nor should any playwright be denied its use if it's in the right context. But this play wasn't the right context. Nor were there any other four letter words in the script. So that the word "fucking" came out as if a different colour to all the rest. There was no pause in the dialogue. Dylan and the other actors were professional enough to keep going at the required pace, but the word seemed to drop into the audience like a depth charge. Had we *really* heard it? Had eight year old Rebecca Hartley, who had battled all day along the wall to be here, heard it? Had those bright and breezy fund-raising Americans heard it? Had all our friends and family heard it? Had Dylan's mother and grandma, and two sisters heard it? I guess they all had.

And at the play's end the distraught Dylan, still unsure how the malevolent two syllables had crept in, rushed up off to our bedroom and locked the door, unable to face fellow actors or playwright father. The poor lad was truly distraught, and needed the reassurances from me, and the rest of the cast, that such moments sometimes happened in live theatre and no matter how professional the approach, no way of preventing such moments completely, and though at the time it may seem the end of the world, soon it would pass into the production's folklore, which of course it soon did.

So that by the next day, one way to guarantee a laugh among the cast as we trudged onwards was to refer to "the fucking Caledonians" moment.

Chapter Six

The Day of the Bull, Hurricane Hadrian and Scattered to the Winds

After the night of triumph, few of us could have predicated the day of disaster.

It was a day that began with our walking party swollen to nine carrying seven flags. By the day's end our numbers would be down to five with only three flags still flying.

Stage manager Craig Davidson has asked to walk with us this day, also Sara of ARTS UK. They, Steve Chettle and the play's director Jackie Fielding were the team that kept us going, they ensured our next accommodation was OK, they prepared the village hall for performance, they saw to our little whims and idiosyncrasies. Steve was building an extensive photographic documentation of the journey and also videoing the play.

We took it for granted everything would be "set" for us, all problems ironed out. And our advance team did meet problems. Such as turning up to a hall to find it locked and no sign of the key holder. Or full of clutter. Or insufficient chairs. We were blissfully ignorant of such mishaps. By the time we arrived everything was sorted.

This was the only day Craig could have walked with us. Any other day, his duties made it impossible. But we had no performance that evening, so he had no setting-up to do. Even so, there was still a good deal of logistics in the seemingly simple matter of one extra body walking alongside us. Craig stayed the night at Twice Brewed. It now meant that Steve Chettle, who had driven the forty miles back to Newcastle late that night, had to drive back the same forty miles early in the morning, follow while Craig drove the van 13 miles to Chollerford, (our next destination), then drive him back the 13 miles to Twice Brewed in time for our 10am start. Only then could he have a cup of tea.

Tuesday was our night of rest before we performed in Humshaugh Village Hall — less than a mile from Chollerford — on the Wednesday. No-one could have predicted just how vital this break would be.

There was a sense of nervous anticipation about us every morning as we prepared to set off. We were like runners before a race, gathered on the road outside Twice Brewed, shaking out our bodies, pacing the ground, eager to be at it. This military road was not the busiest in the world, but being Roman it was dead straight so that what traffic did pass by imitated Michael Schumacher. The fog had cleared and up on the Win Sill we could see the magnificence of the Roman Wall striding out in all its glory.

There was probably more nervousness than usual. We knew this would be our most demanding day's walking. Estimates varied between 12 and 14 miles, but more important, all of these miles would be hard going, our route plunging and soaring with scarcely a yard of flat terrain. In addition to the steep gradients we would face spells of plodging through thick mud.

After the previous day's porous experience with the waterproofs I'd telephoned Dylan's mum Mo, to bring out some replacements to Twice Brewed. These I stuck without checking, in my backpack. Another mistake.

We struck out the short distance along the Military Road in fresh but cloudy conditions, then turned to climb the smaller road up to the wall itself. Half way up this road stood a solitary stone building, seemingly unused. Against the base of the gate was a large rock preventing entrance.

This was the kind of deterrent that made you determined to go in. I climbed the gate to discover the building was called The Peel Bothy, a kind of youth hostel cum shelter. Inscribed on the outer wall was the information that it had been opened by the Queen Mother in 1989.

I thought of the Queen Mum, out here in the middle of nowhere standing in the strong winds which would tug at her monstrous feathered hat, saying to the small gathered crowd of local dignitaries and functionaries "I declare this bothy open," while that same wind blew the vol-au-vents (appropriate really) off the guests' paper plates. I had seen no reference to this building in any Roman Wall book and somehow never associated British Royalty with the Roman Wall. The Queen Mum out here seemed as unlikely as the present queen featuring in my play — hang on though, she did briefly — in a comic cameo from Susie Burton.

People tended to settle into behaviour patterns as the day unfolded. Alex Kinsey often sang, Dave Hollingworth brought up the rear and Bill E. Meeks and Dylan would go charging off at the start setting a searing pace. For some reason Bill drank less water than the rest of us. This was mid-summer, we were putting excessive demands on our bodies with dehydration a definite possibility, and water intake was important. The rest of us glugged it down at regular intervals. Bill seemed to share the W.C. Fields disdain for the stuff, ("Water? That's what fishes fuck in.") And on this day his childlike enthusiasm was missing. That excitable chatter that was part and parcel of Bill E. Meeks was not there. He lagged behind the rest, talking to Craig.

Our first target that day was Housesteads Fort, one of the wall's main settlements, four miles distant. We climbed and dipped, climbed and dipped, foot in front of foot following every contour as we moved through this magnificent if draining scenery. This was a popular section. Although it was isolated, it was reached fairly easily by road from Carlisle or Newcastle. When you thought Roman Wall, it wasn't piddling little piles of stones on the outskirts of Newcastle that came to mind, or the odd few yards east of Carlisle. You thought of these sections. This was the wall proper, this was where it had conquered, and continued to conquer, a fiercely hostile terrain, this was where it was an extraordinary sight, in either the third or twenty-first century. This was what you paid to see. Except it was free. And because this section drew many walkers, the path had been paved and in some places, such as Peel Crags the climb was so steep you were bent forward enough almost to scrape your nose along the paving stones.

On the day's first section we passed what has recently become one of the most famous landmarks hereabouts, yet one which hardly anyone associates with the Roman Wall.

This is the distinctive sycamore tree in sycamore gap, beautifully and symmetrically framed by the perabulae of hills rising each side of it. The tree was made famous in the Kevin Costner Robin Hood film, *Prince of Thieves,* where Costner conversed while sat in its branches. In the film he's supposed to be on his way from Dover to Nottingham, but Hollywood's geographical licence has always been generous.

With delusions of grandeur, Dylan climbed the tree to have his photo taken. But getting down this tree is more difficult than getting up, and he grazed both arms in the process — which was to prove the least troublesome of his day's injuries.

We criss-crossed the wall several times in these early stages, often walking on the northern — or "barbarians" — side. In several places the wall was ten feet high — dramatic enough, but then we got a view of Crag Lough, a natural ice-age lake which you view from the top of terrifyingly sheer cliffs. As you stare down at the lough way below, your stomach lurches, and you think of those young divers seen in travelogues who risk life and limb plunging from dizzy heights into the sea for the benefit (and loot) of the tourists. For some reason the divers are always male. Anyway, no-one was venturing such a plunge here. The wind was fresh and strong and making our flags work overtime in their fierce fluttering. We must have made a distinctive and colourful site in that remote landscape, a small pilgrimage, a winding odyssey, an expedition. But dramatic though the terrain was, and strong though the wind was, the day had still given no hints of the real dramas to come.

Only when we reached Housesteads did we encounter our first problem. Housesteads is "the place of effective fighters", and probably the most visited site along the wall's entire length. To me it lacked the atmosphere and mystery of Birdoswald, but the settlement had generous Roman foundations, wide vistas in all directions, lots of plaques to read, plus an information and gift shop. It was unique in being the only place where you are allowed to walk on the wall itself. This is strictly forbidden elsewhere after years of walkers' feet have caused damage and erosion. The wall authorities are very touchy about this. Prior to our departure a news story in the *Newcastle Evening Chronicle* pictured me standing on the wall at Heddon. I wasn't quite roasted on a spit for the sin, but came pretty close, and as you'll read, I was confronted a couple of days later by an indignant representative of wall authority on the very matter.

We reached Housesteads to discover Bill and Craig had fallen some way behind. This being Craig's first day walking we assumed he was easing himself in, and Bill had chosen to stick with him. We were wrong.

Craig rang us on his mobile — mobile phones had proved an essential on our journey — to tell us Bill was looking (and feeling) decidedly peaky, and he (Craig) was "bringing him in." Now people were arriving at Housesteads in cars, on bikes and buses. They came to stare, to read, to walk, to study. Probably only Bill E. Meeks came to vomit. We waited for Bill and Craig at the site Information Office. Craig was first to show then we spotted Bill. He was staggering down the hill. He resembled an extra from a George Romero film — (*Dawn of the Wall Undead*?) — with a face that altered between the greenness of a processed pea and the whiteness of typing paper. The sprightly optimistic body language had given way to pain and discomfort.

To see Bill E. Meeks without a smile on his face was unusual enough. To see him reduced to this pale-faced inertia was startling. He made his uncertain way past us and behind a Range Rover to throw up as the Twice Brewed breakfast made a second unexpected appearance.

Whatever was wrong with Bill, it was clear that another ten miles of rough steep tracks was not an option for him. In the Information Office, the staff kindly offered to phone for a taxi. Craig would take him to Hexham General Hospital, about 15 miles distant, and after which we'd all play it by ear. It was to prove the end of the day's walking for both Bill and Craig. The taxi took twenty minutes during which time poor Bill died about four times. He had as much energy as an empty bag. The only evidence of life around his person was his flag fluttering energetically in the wind. We tried to rally him, to joke with him, but for once in his life, there was no reciprocal humour from Bill E. Meeks.

The taxi arrived and off they drove. We had no alternative but to carry on walking. Yet how strange it felt to be leaving Housesteads minus one cast member. We fell silent. Our unity had been broken, and at that moment we realised how precious that unity was. We had no idea what ailed Bill, nor if he would be ill for hours, days or weeks. We had no stand-ins. What if he were told to rest for a week? How would anyone perform the part of Cogno?

We walked off into the unknown, and where we had been nine at the start of the day, we were now down to seven. Which before too long was to become six.

East of Housesteads we were climbing a steep hill alongside the wall when ahead of us we heard a loud, somewhat tortured noise. It emanated from a very large, very black, and very bad-tempered looking bull. Bulls are not known for their lyrical tones. It's a fair assumption a bull is totally tone deaf such is unmusicality of their bellowing. Nor does a bull ever seem in a good temper. This bull was stood at right angles to the wall, directly in our path. We were on open grass land, and a long way from any refuge.

The next few moments now seem blurred. I remember someone's phone rang and it was Jackie Fielding to say Bill was safely at Hexham General and was undergoing tests. As I was speaking to her, I realised the formidable black beast was lumbering towards Dylan in a way to suggest he (the bull) wasn't just looking for a sugar lump.

"Hang on a minute Jackie," I said, "Dylan's being chased by a bull."

"Oh, tell him to stop mucking about," she said, obviously believing this was all a bit of a prank. It wasn't. The bull had now gathered speed, and was pursuing Dylan towards the wall at an angle that made it difficult for him to escape.

Except via one route. Whether his action was brave or foolhardy is open to conjecture. But he dived head-first over that historic monument rather like an Olympic swimmer diving to start the 100 metres freestyle. I can picture the arc of this dive perfectly. It takes a deal of provocation to dive unseen over a large stone wall with no knowledge what is on the other side. A large muscular black angry bull *is* that sort of provocation. The dive was partially successful in that it got him to the other side of the wall. Total success was denied by two factors. Firstly when he sat up in the field on the wall's north side he realised he was staring into the large eyes of a second bull (this one a more whitish or light brown colour).

It had been some disagreement between these two massive beasts, one each side of the wall, that had produced Blackie's bad temper to start with and led it to chase Dylan. The bulls were clearly having a stand-off. So that here, across the Roman Wall where centuries before,

Romans and Caledonians had been sworn enemies, the hostilities were now played out by two bulls. And in the middle was Dylan.

He was lucky that bull number two had obviously been on some anger management course. Or maybe it was of a more sympathetic nature than Blackie. Whatever, the beast simply stared at the young man who'd landed beneath it, and exhaled down its rubbery nostrils.

Now the second factor denying total success. When Dylan stood up to make good his escape he realised the dive had damaged his foot, through it would probably have taken a leg amputation at that moment to prevent him making his good his departure. He clambered back on top of the wall ("Hey, you! Get off that ancient monument!") and was relieved to find that by this time the black bull had lost interest, and trundled off to a part of the field which allowed us all free passage.

The bulls had been staring at one another across the wall as we approached and when we looked back some 200 yards later they had taken up the same position again. At the hilltop we rested and warned walkers going east to west of the possible hazard ahead. There was a fatalistic compulsion in watching these other unfortunates as they approached the bothersome beast, which luckily stayed close to the wall, allowing them to give it a wide berth and escape with all limbs intact.

Only then did it strike me that Dylan was carrying a large conspicuous, and very red, flag. Experts are certain that the whole red flag/bull affair is a myth, and that it is movement not colour that attracts the animal. Everyone knows this, except perhaps the bulls.

Two miles later we stopped to eat our sandwiches, slightly shell-shocked. The sky was darkening and though Dylan's foot had initially seemed to improve now it was worsening, and he walked with a pronounced limp. We offered to carry his back-pack.

"I'll just walk it off," he said, but it wasn't to prove that simple.

"Look," I said, "don't walk on it if it's giving you bother. We'll sort something out."

"I came here to walk the Roman Wall," he said, "so that's what I want to do."

And that's what he did *try* to do, though as the afternoon proceeded, other matters impinged, and it became clear that for Dylan also further progress on this day was impossible.

Two men down already, one suspect, and if the truth were known at this stage none of us gave a toss about the Roman Wall, and we were to give even less of a toss fairly soon. After Swingshields Crags, the spectacular terrain of the previous two days began to flatten out, and the going become less arduous. At least on one level. But as we crossed what seemed a limitless field which offered not a single square inch of protection, we spotted moving towards us from the far side a huge rain cloud.

Unlike the city, in the countryside you can often see the weather approaching. This cloud though was particularly unusual as it seemed to move almost at ground level. It reminded me of the cloud that enveloped Grant Williams in the 1957 film *The Incredible Shrinking Man*, eventually turning him to the size of a pinhead. Except that cloud was white. And this one was as black as a bull. It was moving inexorably towards us, and no escaping it.

Janine Birkett, in what was to prove one of the tour's great understatements, said, "Looks like we're in for some rain."

We were about to encounter what I nicknamed Hurricane Hadrian. We stopped to don our waterproofs. I had the new ones which had been brought out to Steel Rigg the night before. When I unpacked these I found they were in fact two identical thin plastic capes, poncho style, with the words THE BANK OF SCOTLAND printed on in large white letters. There were no waterproof trousers.

The cape fastened with a baffling series of press-studs. On each of the first three attempts the studs and holes never matched up and the cape sat on me at an odd angle.

I had more or less conquered one of the capes when the rain started, and I had to put my faith in the Bank of Scotland.

It began as rapidly and as fiercely as a domestic power-shower. The rain hurled down with such ferocity that we suspected that cloud of being demonically possessed. Within seconds water was running off us in great torrents. My cape kept a small part of me partly dry for a few moments, but the rain ran off the bottom and onto my trackie bottoms so rapidly and fiercely that within minutes their weight was tripled and they began to sag. They slid down over my hips and would have been round my knees had I not yanked them up.

This rain was so fierce that later I found a notebook in an inner pocket turned to mush. Alex Kinsey had a packet of polo mints in his pocket and the storm simply liquidised them. There was nothing we could do except keep going. Each of us in turn shouted something into the wind and rain which no-one else heard. The rain came in huge flapping flags across the open land. We had no protection; either by staying still or moving, so moving seemed preferable. The rain was of tropical intensity and though the storm lasted only ten minutes it brought with it devastation and saturation. It was the kind of exposure we urbanites never had to face; in the unlikely event of us experiencing such rain we could nip into the shelter of a shop or pub till it blew over. And because cities had rendered the elements (temporarily) fairly irrelevant, we falsely believed we had domain over them. Recent events in the likes of New Orleans, or the tsunami showed this up for the hubris it was, and we were all slowly realising the truth — that us lot are merely playthings.

When the big black cloud had done its worst with us, and taken its leave, we slumped onto a stretch of the Roman Wall (bugger the rules) to take stock. No-one spoke for a time, then a mobile rang. It was news from Hexham General Hospital, and the timing was superb. Right at that moment when we had almost been washed away, when extremes of water had laid siege to us and our feeble "waterproofs", came the news that Bill E. Meeks was suffering from dehydration, was on an intravenous drip and could well be detained overnight. Dylan's foot meantime was killing him.

It was probably our darkest hour, but as is the way at such moments, a small miracle happened. It did nothing to alleviate our situation in any practical way, but it slightly lifted our spirits. Across the field, and spreading into the next one, low down and perfectly formed so that you could have gone up to stroke them, appeared not one, but two magnificent rainbows. A brace of rainbows, one nudged up behind the other!

And this was what the rainbows seemed to be telling us, that if we townies *did* come out here and have the audacity to take on the elements, then those elements might feel the need to show us this countryside was not all just picture postcard views; it could be cruel and savage as well. As it just had been, but hey — no hard feelings, and here's a double rainbow to cheer you up again!

To say we were "cheered up" would be something of an exaggeration. This day was ripping us apart, it was scattering us like chaff, a soaked ragbag, a sopping disarray of a theatre company. Our flags were dripping wet, our waterproofs shot to hell, Dylan was unable to walk much further and we were still three miles short of that night's destination.

We phoned Craig. The situation with Ill Bill was still unclear. OK, could Craig now come and collect Dylan in the company van and drive him to the same Hexham General Hospital which rapidly was filling up with Cloud Nine actors? To look on the bright side for Ill Bill, he had at least missed the deluge. We were able to read the half-saturated map and arrange a rendezvous with Craig half a mile distant where the wall crossed a minor road. He arrived and took away Dylan and one sopping flag. Plus Alex's flag which had broken in the deluge. Flags and actors were disappearing at a rapid rate. The centre could not hold. And secretly we all wanted to jump in that van, just be warm and safe and at our destination, but it was not yet to be. Now three of our members were absent, but no, it was four, because Susie Burton was gone too. But where? How?

We phoned her mobile. She had gone off ahead on her own while we waited around for the van. She was tired and fed-up and couldn't hang around. Her tone was definitely pissed off, and her only ambition was to reach Chollerford as soon as possible.

So there was about us was a sense of things falling apart, disintegrating. Our famous unity had been found wanting. The entire crew was exhausted. We had all had enough of this day. We were soaked through and cold, and dispirited, and already it was way the past our normal time of arriving at our evening destination.

Here was a small event of some significance. On the afternoon's journey we passed the sign to a Mithraic Temple (Mithraism having been the main religion of the Romans). We'd said earlier how we'd like to make the short detour to see this temple. Yet the only reaction once we reached the sign was that the temple could go stuff itself. And here was another irony. Guess which animal is central to the whole Mithraic religion? A bull.

By the last mile of this day Janine had dropped back on her own, Dave was also isolated and the main group was a damp huddle numbering a pathetic three, myself, Alex and Sara from ARTS UK. We didn't speak on this mile because we had nothing to say. The mile felt endless; we had boots that squelched, clothes that were wet through and chafing against cold skin.

We walked or dragged ourselves into the small village of Chollerford and the foyer of the George Hotel, where we laid down our dripping wet flags, plonked down on the carpeted floor our saturated backpacks and cagoules. Small pools of water formed around them.

"We are the Cloud Nine Theatre Company," I said, adding, "or at least what's left of them."

The receptionist took all this in her stride, handed out room keys and announced, "Dinner is from 7pm."

There were still jokes to be played on us by the fates. We took our keys, our soaked flags and packs, and made our way towards the hotel rooms. The George at Chollerford has the longest corridors of any hotel in the world. They are endless and labyrinthine and bear no relationship to logic, so that you pass by room 312 and then find room 178. There are rumours that some guests have been wandering these corridors for years, feeding off the odd scraps left on trays outside doors. Our pedometer (which had escaped the deluge unharmed), announced that we had already walked 13.4 miles on this day, had taken 27,294 steps and burned (if you can use the verb in such non-flammable conditions) 948 calories. It seemed the corridors of The George Hotel were determined to see those figures doubled.

Let us look on the bright side. The George was a magnificent location, the beautifully landscaped gardens gently sloping down to the soft-flowing North Tyne where (in better conditions) you could sit and sip afternoon tea and view the splendid stone bridge that bestrode the river. The elegant stone hotel had its own swimming pool and sauna. It was our most luxurious stop of the journey, and though our spirits and energy levels were low, fate had smiled on us in that this being our one night off we did not have to perform again for more than 24 hours. Actors could do a lot of recharging in 24 hours. Plus which there was good news on the injury front. Both our two unfortunates had now returned from Hexham General Hospital. While confined, Ill Bill had been put on a saline drip, but was not required to stay in overnight. He was told to take it easy and still looked severely drained. Dylan had damaged a ligament in his foot, but *not* severely, and the next day's rest should see it OK. I found him sat in the hotel bar cheekily supping a pint of lager.

One of Ill Bill's theories was that he (Bill) had been victim of hallucogenic sheep shit. None of us could quite put this theory together, except that it had to do with him gathering and eating mushrooms en route, some of which may have been magic, and some of which may have been visited by sheep.

There was the small matter of the main gent's toilet in the George and the lack of loo roll. The loo roll was missing when we arrived and despite three complaints at reception, it was still *in absentio* when we left 39 hours later. This lack of loo roll meant that any males caught short in the hotel's general area faced the major expedition through the corridors back to their own room for relief. Things could have been nasty.

The George had once been privately owned but was now part of a large chain, a fact that, despite it being an impressive building and location imbued it with a corporate feel, that lack of individuality of hotels run to the policies of some distant head office. I had no idea who the manager was, nor if s/he had any personality. There was no sense of *mein host*, only young fresh-faced barmen who seemed to interact as per some company handbook. They put the bar shutters up bang on closing time, unlike most flexible rural drinking holes. Plus which we were residents.

Corporate or not, The George had its own swimming pool, and after such a day, to slide into its comforting waters was close to nirvana. I shut my eyes, thought of that big black cloud, thought of Dylan diving across the wall, thought of Ill Bill vomiting behind the Range Rover, and wondered if the RSC ever had these problems when they took a show on the road.

I was doubling up that night with Dave Hollingworth. Dave was the quietest of our group. I didn't know him very well personally and he was so convincing on stage as the ruthless entrepreneur Loot, I assumed that beneath this quiet he was a hard nut. In fact he was the gentlest of men, and his story was to prove a tragic one.

I was carrying with me the paraphernalia of a writer working on the hoof; various note books, reference book, pens, bottles of ink, photocopies of articles and other bits of junk. These I kept close to my person at all times, tucked into the back of my waterproof backpack. I say waterproof but I may as well claim dynamite is flameproof. The backpack was simply no match for Hurricane Hadrian. At the bottom of the pack a small pool of water had now gathered and most of the contents were in a sorry state. This necessitated me drying out some vital information, and recarpeting the entire room with soggy pieces of paper, damp research articles, and notebooks where the ink was often blurred. Poor Dave, his leisure space was taken over and he had to tiptoe round the room. All the documents eventually dried, and in so doing became the consistency of a Ryvita wafer. Somehow I managed to write that evening's article.

Getting it over to *The Journal* was another matter. I requested use of the hotel computer, this being simpler than using the accursed lap-top. I sat at the back of hotel reception, typed in the new version of the 850 words, and asked if I could e-mail it.

"Oh, sorry," said the receptionist, "you can't send any emails after 7pm from here." The time was 7.10pm.

She was unaware why this strange ban on evening emails existed. Nor was there much point pursuing the reason.

They had a fax machine. So I went to Plan B — print the article off and fax it over to the newspaper. "I'm afraid the printer is out of order."

My article was trapped inside the computer. I could see it on the screen but it may as well have been on Mars. One possibility was set-up the lap-top and retype the entire article then try to send it down the line. My heart sank at the possible pitfalls of this option.

Time was running out. The newspaper liked the piece to be sent over by 7.30. Plus which I wanted some grub. I felt chained to these daily articles, a prisoner of the play's diary. Almost every evening this activity of filing the article gave me grief in one form or another. But whose fault was that? I *had* wanted to write them, after all.

I had a sudden thought. Back in the 70s and 80s I had worked for *The Journal*. I had sent over by phone various travel articles and theatre reviews, dictated to what they called "copy', a man specially trained for the task wearing headphones and sat at a keyboard. I feared technology may have now done away with this system, but on a whim rang the normal *Journal* number, and said "Give me copy please."

There was a click, then a voice said, "copy". No, it was not just a voice; it was *that* voice, the very same voice I had dictated to dozens of times a third of a century ago.

"Hang on a second," I said, "is that Sandy?"

"Yes it is."

"The same Sandy who took down my articles from 1974 onwards, starting with *Travels with a Donkey*?"

"The very same. And you must be Peter Mortimer."

"That's right. And you're still taking copy Sandy!"

"Yes I am. And you're still dictating it."

"Yes, I am."

I imagined Sandy taking copy through all the Thatcher years, the fall of the Berlin Wall, global warming, the twin towers. There was something reassuring about this, as there also was in indulging once again the rituals of dictating my article, using all the jargon such as "open par", "close par," "upper and lower", "full out," "open speech marks," "space", and the ultimate instruction "stop and end." And now I had a safety net, the knowledge that in the middle of all this unpredictable hi-tech, Sandy was sat somewhere in the bowels of Thomson House in Newcastle wearing his headphones. I decided there and then, that the hi-tech could go to hell. I would dictate all future articles via Sandy. Here was the plan. Write version one freehand. Type it onto the laptop, then read if off the screen to Sandy. And if this seemed a ridiculous process to technophiles, so be it. Dictation took about 25 minutes. Sandy and I were reunited. Even though I had never once laid eyes on him.

By the time I'd filed copy, I felt exhausted. It was a battle-scarred *Cloud Nine* outfit that came down to dinner in The George that night.

The hotel's usual clientele was fairly elderly and sedate, people who paid good money for peace and pampering. In the midst of which our own ragbag party looked slightly conspicuous. We were though much more reserved than normal. Our usual high spirits were diluted 80 per cent. Bill Meeks hardly opened his mouth either to speak or eat. He ordered a succulent steak and when it arrived simply looked at it. So as not to leave a mess, I ate it. Susie, Alex, Janine, Dylan and Dave spent much time looking at the tablecloth. We had survived the day but the day's torments still had a hold on us. We felt drained, rung-out, de-energised to the extent that ever again having the vitality and energy to perform a high-paced play seemed unlikely in the extreme.

In the quiet tasteful dining room waiters glided back and forth offering silver service. Steve Chettle had come out to dine with us and did his best to cheer us by providing free wine. His assistant Sara was still with us, though our brave stage manager Craig, who had ferried our injured hither and thither had already gone back to Newcastle.

On this day we had passed through some of the Roman Wall's most spectacular countryside. Yet for most of the day we'd been miserable and even when the wild terrain had flattened out, the extreme rain had turned many field entrances into almost impassable thick cloying mud. We sat quietly in the bar after the meal. I bought the last round — five drinks. I handed over £20, which was still 10p short. I felt stung.

The beds at The George were soft and luxurious. Dave Hollingworth was already asleep. Things began to fall back as I stretched out, and despite all the bad images of the day as I drifted into sleep, it was the magic double rainbow that came into my vision.

Chapter Seven

Staying Put, Giant Chess and a Village Reception

Most people who walk the Roman Wall do so east to west, and most guide books are written with east-west as the assumed route. This was little use to us, and we often had to refer to these publications backwards. Should you want to do it west-east, like us, then one book you can use is *Hadrian's Wall Today* published by Tynedale Council.

The reasons for East-West dominating are historical. The numbering of the wall castles has been done starting at Wallsend, so that's where people tend to begin, at the numerical beginning. Doing it east-west also means you get the wonderful huge landscapes of the Solway Firth for the climax, followed by a decent pint in Bowness and the chance to write a bit of Latin in the Roman Wall book at The King's Arms.

Though this direction does leave you a long way from a regular transport system (there are occasional buses from Bowness to Carlisle). Plus which the prevailing winds are west-east, which means they are in your face if you travel east-west. On days such as the one previous this may simply mean the torrential rain penetrates the back of your waterproof quicker than the front. Surprisingly enough no-one seems quite sure in which direction the wall itself was built; general opinion is that it was constructed in lots of different bits that eventually joined up, like a puzzle.

One seasoned walker, in favour of our own direction, said, "the trouble with walking east to west is that by the time you've covered 13 miles of Tyneside tarmac you've probably got blisters already and without yet seeing even a glimpse of any wall." Footwise, west-east is probably the better option.

I woke the next morning in the soft bed. Dave Hollingworth in the bed opposite was making snurgle noises and I let him be. Drifting into my mind came a small incident after the Twice Brewed performance which I'd totally forgotten in all the excitement of that heady night.

I'd been approached by a stern looking official of some Hadrian's Wall organisation who had reprimanded me for being photographed in the newspaper on the wall itself. This he said could encourage others to do the same, and hasten the wall's deterioration. In the true tradition of the first wall walker/writer William Hutton, who often got his notes mixed up or failed to take down details, I likewise failed to get this official's name.

I ate humble pie, agreed the wall needed protecting and that sitting on it for a photo had been an oversight, and I promised him I would find a way of mentioning the matter in my daily column for *The Journal*. I felt like a chastised schoolboy, but waking this morning the criticism I realised wasn't all one way.

The Roman Wall had been declared a National Trail in 2003 amid a blaze of publicity. This attracted global attention, and it was obvious the site was attracting visitors from throughout the planet. The numbers of walkers has increased dramatically since 2003. Some came to walk the whole length; others came out for a Sunday stroll of a few miles on the most spectacular middle section.

While some of the wall was well prepared with planking and paths specially treated, other parts were dreadful. On the previous day, especially near the field gates, we were often ankle deep in mud with a surface more in keeping with the Battle of the Somme. No-one could predict the weather, but there seemed to have been no regard in these places for a walker's well-being. A few boards would not have gone amiss.

Plus which the Roman Wall was not Pamplona, and people were entitled to feel relatively safe while enjoying its delights. I knew no-one who relished being chased by a bull, and having these large forbidding and dangerous animals close to where people walked and with no protection in between seemed like an accident waiting to happen — as one just had. Luckily the only damage had been an injured foot. Bulls could cause much worse injury than that.

The writer Hunter Davies, three decades ago had complained about the lack of hotel and catering facilities along the wall. You could see his point, but short of turning into some kind of nightmare theme park (which incidentally was the plot of my play) it was difficult to know what to do. I suspected that for most walkers, the isolation was part of the attraction, and they may have been slightly miffed to come across a Harry Ramsden's at every other mile castle.

In my play I thought I was taking the wall as a vehicle to write a satire on modern Britain, though director Jackie Fielding said to me "actually it's a love story at heart" and maybe she was right. When we end up writing exactly what we expected to write at the start, it's usually a bad sign. Plus which in theatre everything eventually springs from character, no matter what specific issue angrily motivates you to write in the first place.

Though the more I got involved with writing the play the more fascinating the Roman Wall became (apparently Roman Wall addicts are not an uncommon species). What once had been a brutal frontier was now a "safe" piece of heritage, and I wondered if people would in time come to view Israel's wall on the West Bank in the same light? As this was built in concrete it would probably crumble in a quarter of the time of Hadrian's creation.

At one stage in my play, Loot, the entrepreneur and main character says, "that's what Britain likes isn't it, the old, the ruined, the tumbledown?" This is probably true, but I also liked the fact the wall had resisted commercialisation and commodification. Strangely enough since the play was produced, there have been moves to bring it under single ownership, and there could also be involvement of an organisation with links to a theme park. So life could perhaps soon be imitating art.

The last thing I wanted was for the wall to be over-civilised. Then neither did I want its visitors to risk being chased by an angry bull through thick mud.

This was a day of recuperation. We weren't required to travel anywhere, unless you discounted the one mile from The George up the hill to Humshaugh Village Hall, where we would perform that evening and where apparently, all tickets had been sold.

I was not used to having no agenda. I had far too many agendas in my life, and needed to chill out more. Here was the perfect opportunity. There was something quite delicious about facing no mileage on this day. The company drifted down to breakfast in drabs. Already we had put some of the previous day's nightmares behind us, and I could sense people recovering their strength and energy.

Alex Kinsey would have his flag repaired on this day, which would symbolise our recuperation. Only poor Bill still seemed out of sorts. We were used to Bill Meeks bouncing into each day with an infectious enthusiasm. He'd crack ten jokes while most people were still in their first yawn. His infectious laughter and beaming face streaked through with a childlike delight just to be alive, was part of our group's fortitude.

On this morning it was not so much Ill Bill as Still Bill. He looked better than the walking corpse of the previous day, but he was reserved. He did not gesticulate wildly, nor break out into sudden gales of laughter. He ate his breakfast with the sobriety a travelling salesman would show before going off with his case full of samples.

Yet we still had ten hours before performance. There was no way Bill Meeks would not get out there and do his stuff. Dylan was still limping, but less so. He was young, and confident the temporary injury would not affect his performance, or his walking the next day.

How blessed we were to have the previous night and this day free. How impossible things would have been without this break. We ate breakfast without one eye on the clock, without needing mentally to prepare ourselves for a long trudge ahead. There were tons to eat. You served yourself from those large silver platters with huge domed lids that made a clattering noise when you replaced them, so that a symphony of light background clatter was always in the background as we ate. One logistical problem was how to get the bacon and sausage on your plate while still using one hand to hold those giant lids, for there was nowhere to put them down except back on the platter itself.

And thus, in various ways throughout this day, the members of Cloud Nine recuperated. Dave Hollingworth had once worked on the Roman Wall, and went off to nearby Hexham to look up old buddies. For some reason this foray unnerved me, as if someone going off like this broke the chain of our journey and might bring bad luck or affect our behaviour. It did neither and when Dave returned he had a present for me, a book of short stories by the author Garrison Kiellor, who we both liked and whose work we had talked about en route.

Many of us spent a good deal of time in and around the swimming pool. There was a giant chess board in the garden and I gave Dylan a game, totally throwing him by my employment of the Nimzovitch defence. For some reason the black knight was missing and my shoulder bag had to stand in. We needed to break off from the game at one stage and when we returned someone had moved the pieces around, so Dylan was spared the final humiliation.

Our clothes were a total mess. Not for the first or last time our indefatigable stage manager Craig Davidson came to the rescue, taking the whole bundle off to the nearest laundrette, which was some miles away in Haltwhistle (laundrettes were a bit thin on the ground in rural Northumberland). And already en route from Newcastle was our equally indefatigable costumier Meriel Johnston who would spend most of that day ironing and freshening up the jaded costumes, ready for the evening performance.

Humshaugh, which was an idyllic stone village, was bathed this day in gentle sunshine. This was a welcome antidote to the ferocious weather of the day previous. The village had an attractive small school, a village shop, neat grassy verges, and in the local, The Crown Hotel, lunches cost only £2.75, even if the menu featured just three items.

Humshaugh was the kind of peaceful village where you would stand in the centre, look around you, breathe deeply and be absolutely and utterly convinced that somewhere in this rural idyll, someone would be plotting to murder someone else. Humshaugh Village Hall seated 107. If you took this sell-out figure, related it to the size of the village, extrapolated these statistics to Tyneside, a similar sell-out audience would number around 100,000. Nice to dream anyway. The smaller the locale, the more likely a high percentage of the population would turn out. This was because the sense of occasion was much stronger in a small community.

One hundred people squeezed into a village hall gave me a bigger buzz than two thousand reclining in a posh theatre, but unlike a posh theatre many of these places had no existing mechanism for marketing and selling a live play. It was down to ARTS UK in each of the nine venues to find reliable and supportive people, who could take on the often arduous task to "educate" the village population that it should buy a ticket and turn up, even though Coronation Street or East Enders might just have taken on a brand new plot line.

Many of our audience would be seeing live theatre for the first time, which was exciting but daunting. And who was to say whether our visit would be a roaring success, or we'd fall flat on our faces in front of empty rows of seats? I had always been fearful about enquiring over advance ticket sales at any of my plays, the secret dread being that the single word reply would be "none".

But our audiences were increasing, and we were meeting more and more people along the wall trail who had heard about us, were reading about us in the newspapers, and were actually planning to see us.

All of which could make you feel the centre of the universe, a common enough delusion for anyone immersed in some creative venture. That the majority of the population would not see, nor even much care about our project did not cross our minds, nor should it have. Every writer, painter, musician, actor, theatre company or orchestra needs this delusion to power them on and whatever the evidence to the contrary — of which there was a considerable amount — I had to go believing that Cloud Nine's activities were of huge significance, and I didn't even want to consider how few people would flock to our play compared to the numbers tuning in for the National Lottery numbers.

The village hall in Humshaugh left me optimistic. Not only the full house, also the sense the building was well cared for, the bright new paintwork, plus the warm welcome. A whole clutch of volunteers was on hand to ensure our evening was a success. These were all female, all aged over fifty, because that is the sex and age group that run important things such as village halls, and maybe we should give them a go at running the country, though probably they'd have more sense than to want to.

As we grew closer to Tyneside, so more friends and colleagues were in the audiences. This night we'd see the poets Linda France and Ellen Phethean, plus the crime writer David Belbin. We were also to be given an "official reception" in the village.

Humshaugh was the home of the renowned children's writer David Almond, whose work has swept up almost every prize going (start with the brilliant *Skellig* if by any chance you haven't read him). I published two collections of David's short stories before he was visited by fame, and he and his partner Sara-Jane Palmer laid on food and drinks for the entire Cloud Nine crew after the show. They lived with their daughter Freya Grace in the kind of beautiful old stone house with large gardens at the edge of the village where you'd imagine an Agatha Christie murder. David told me he would sometimes stand in this garden, look around and think back to his time growing up on Leam Lane Council estate in Gateshead, an upbringing that has informed much of his writing, but which was very different to Humshaugh.

The village hall filled rapidly, and there was a buzz as the house lights went down. I jumped up and announced that night's singer Ruth Lambert, who was accompanied by a young violinist Hannah Rickard. Probably nowhere in England has such a strong folk song tradition as the North-East (a tradition that has been bolstered and strengthened by the work of the *Folkworks* agency located at Sage Music Centre). A whole clutch of well-worn songs were known (and occasionally drunkenly sung) by the majority of the population, and Ruth and Hannah picked out a few to warm up the audience, *The Morpeth Rant*, *The Lambton Worm*, ending with a nerve tingling and plaintive version of the beautiful song *The Water of Tyne*. This rendition saw more than a few handkerchiefs pulled out of bags and pockets; by the time the play went up the audience were putty in our hands.

I was excited about this performance but also apprehensive. This was the sixth time we'd done the play but since leaving Bowness on Solway, we'd never had a gap between performances. A piece of theatre could go off the boil rapidly. Even five per cent deterioration in timing, energy and delivery became obvious, especially in a piece so finely tuned as this. A theatre production was a living organic thing, the sum of its many complex parts. It was a product of the human imagination, and though technology had its role to play, on the night the success or failure was usually down to human attributes. A theatre piece was a striving for perfection by imperfect beings, a coming together of many different people, personalities and backgrounds who in unison hoped to create something important, something that transcended all our normal human fallibilities. Or at least for me it was all of these things. For some it might just have been about earning a crust.

A live theatre performance was not totally predictable, like a film which was safely housed on celluloid and could not alter from one showing to the next. But because it had a pre-ordained script and structure, neither was a play as unpredictable as a football match or any other sporting event. And somewhere in that carefully planned, minutely honed, but unpredictable nature, lay its fascination.

How would it end up at Humshaugh? It began slightly off-pace, and I could tell Bill Meeks, who dropped a couple of lines, was still not 100 per cent. But both he and the play recovered as it worked up a head of steam, as if with each line and scene the traumas of the previous day receded more, confidence grew till finally the cast took their bow to enthusiastic applause. I loved Jane Holman's songs. I hated the artificiality of stage musicals, the way the form interfered with a natural dramatic flow, how everything stopped for the big number. So *Off the Wall* was in no way a musical, yet it included music, which needed to dovetail effortlessly, and to be as dramatic as normal dialogue. Jane's musical direction meant that when Dave Hollingworth as Loot sang the rapacious *Everything is for Sale*, or engaged in musical conflict with his wife, played by Janine Birkett in *The Oil Song*, the style and delivery didn't render the characters unreal. Bill Meeks had suffered on stage. Quietly (and he was not normally the most taciturn of men), he made his way back to the hotel, declining to attend the local or David and Sara-Jane's get-together.

One of the nightly delights for the cast was the pub gathering post-show (and here, pre-buffet). Actors are as keen for praise as writers, and in these small communities our play was a big event in the calendar. We were conspicuous in the small rural pubs, and flattering comments often came in spades. People who didn't like it, I presumed kept quiet. The bar of the Crown Hotel was packed, and we were the centre of attention. Actors who feign shyness and even irritation at such attention are faking it, and being untrue to themselves. I have never known one actor who deep down did not want to be recognised and praised, be it by a posh theatre critic, some woman in a supermarket queue, or the regulars in The Crown Hotel, Humshaugh. And heavens, why shouldn't they? What actor goes through all that work and discipline from the desire to be ignored? Who doesn't want to be loved and appreciated?

A slight sense of the melancholic was on me that evening; I knew we had now passed the wall's finest stretches, and that although we faced a steep drag up from Chollerford the next morning from hereon the landscape mainly would begin to flatten,. The countryside would become tamer. I knew also our days in this strange peripatetic way of life were limited; these seven people tumbled together in an extraordinary way, walking, eating, sleeping and performing very much in one another's pockets.

I'd switched on the TV news in the Chollerford hotel room and saw some human tragedy in Falluja, Iraq. I had to switch it off. Too much reality, as it's been said, is unbearable. I wanted to stay with the Roman Wall, to be on it, to respond to it, to be walking alongside it .The ugliness of real life seemed alien to me at that moment; I wanted what small-scale theatre in rural locations brought and I couldn't contemplate being away from the Wall, that one-time symbol of brutal repression which was now to me a spiritual crutch. For three years we had been planning this theatrical venture and now that it was upon us, I wanted to cling to it. I felt a great affection towards the cast and the rest of the team. I didn't want them go away and dissolve in the manner all theatre casts did after the final performance. I knew there would be that sense of emptiness at the end because this was an inevitable part of the way of life, but I didn't want to think of it, because the thought brought me down.

Now all of this melodramatic gushing may well have been down to the several large glasses of white wine I put down at Dave & Sara-Jane's house later that night. Or maybe I was taking the belief that theatre could change people's lives to its inevitable conclusions. Except wasn't it supposed to be the audiences whose lives were changed, not the playwright's?

Chapter Eight

TV Stars, Drama under Canvas and the Heavens Open Again

A play allows you to do just what is says — to play. This is not the same as to work. Play may be just as demanding as work, but to play entails doing something for creative as against productive or materialistic reasons. No society can get by without either the play or the work element, but our own society tends to have relegated play to a more minor role than work. This can be seen in various ways. Education is not a means to an end, a learning process that makes of the individual a more complete person, but something harnessed to productive and economic requirements. Culture is regularly assessed in the amount of foreign tourist and income it might bring in. Which means that any culture that does not turn a fast buck (and much of it doesn't) is deemed as inferior. Economic progress can be measured in statistics. Spiritual and creative progress is more difficult. Hence politicians stick to the former, proclaim its superiority and attempt to make it a self-fulfilling prophesy, which in many ways they have done. It is now many years since I decided to devote my life and energies to play rather than work. Say this to anyone and they assume you are a frivolous person, which again shows the misconception of play. I'm often totally exhausted and drained from this dedication to play. It takes far more energy discipline and dedication than what I did previously. But I have no intention of going back to work.

And people who went to see a theatre piece probably never analysed just why they should make the journey to observe people they didn't know pretend to be other people they didn't know. (I wish I'd thought of that analysis first, but alas, the dues belong to someone else). But they did do this, and by so doing expressed the importance of play. And it seemed extraordinary that we were now walking the entire width of the country, taking on foot our piece of theatre to remote venues and inviting the local populace to come and join us for an evening, and what's more they were turning up! There was no compulsion for them to come, nor was there any easily quantifiable benefit outside of observing this group of people at play. Except there was no reason it should seem extraordinary at all. Not if we fully understood the relevance of play.

There was very little to Chollerford, considering everyone in the North-East knew of it, whereas Humshaugh, just up the hill and much bigger was hardly known at all. Why was this? Maybe it was the presence of The George in Chollerford, considered one of the poshest hotels in the region (with, or without loo roll — of which there was still no sign when we left).

Most of Chollerford was clustered round one traffic island and a road junction. For reasons I couldn't understand this small settlement had two garages; it also had a handful of houses, plus The George, plus an impressive looking stud (not a gigolo, a horse-breeding centre) a stone road bridge across the River Tyne. And a few hundred yards along the river the remains of one of the Roman Wall's most spectacular original bridges. There was not a great deal to look at once you ferreted out this relic, but if you persevered with close attention to detail, you would come across a rather fine and perfectly preserved phallus in the stonework, a fact which may or may not be of great interest to you.

Despite its length, the Roman Wall traverses only three rivers, the Tyne the Irthing and the Eden. Nor is it crossed by many roads, this being such a remote region. Despite its great popularity, Hadrian's Wall has managed to retain an impressive sense of isolation, a feeling that the presence of visitors crawling along its length is a matter of supreme indifference to it. Maybe this is why, that despite being a two thousand year old line of old rock, it would always have a fascination the likes of Alton Towers, desperate for attention, could never achieve.

Ill Bill was back to his sprightly self this morning, and Dylan the Limp also seemed recovered. Our journey was nine miles to the Robin Hood Inn which was situated at — well not really at anywhere. The Robin Hood was on a long isolated stretch of the Military Road (built on top of the wall). The villages of Matfen and Whittingham lay to the West, and the odd farm was scattered about, but the population was sparse.

It would be a unique experience for us, as we were to perform in a large marquee. The Robin Hood was the only feasible place within miles to perform, but had no room big enough to house both the play and a decent audience. We were assured that early in the summer a permanent marquee was to be erected in the field at the back, and thus we thought our problems were over.

But no. This marquee never materialised. Planning permission was turned down. We were then left, a few weeks prior to the tour with several options. Change plans; walk on another six or seven miles and book somewhere suitable. This got a quick thumbs down as by this time the whole itinerary had been planned and in any event it made for too long a walking day.

We could perform *al fresco* and pray heartily for blessing from the sun god and put a total ban on rain dancing. This option also was dismissed. An outdoor performance required totally different disciplines. Props could blow away, voices needed more projection, the audience this far north could freeze to death, lighting required different programming, plus which our electrics were designed for inside use, and exposure to the wet could be dangerous.

The only reasonable alternative was to sort out our own overnight marquee. This was a big job and costly, but ARTS UK gritted their teeth and organised it.

Again a marquee that would be suitable for a wedding would not necessarily suit our play. Hard to get black-out for one thing, there was virtually no sound insulation from the nearby road, and what about the surface of the field? We would need to use wooden boarding to build a stage, but to create any sort of surface more ambitious than matting for the spectators would be prohibitively expensive, and we had no idea if chairs would simply sink in through the matting and soil.

No matter. There were several pluses to the day; the journey of nine miles on a fairly flat terrain was unlikely to hold many terrors for us super-lithe, fit band of players. It was a gentle stroll, an amble round the block. We could probably have walked it backwards.

Nor did there seem much danger of major dissent in the ranks. There were petty annoyances (I threatened to strangle Alex Kinsey if he sang one more time a song which he failed to realise had highly unpleasant fascist connections). There were times you wanted to speak to no-one and trudged alone. But we were mercifully spared major personality or health problems. Our three weeks of surgical spirit foot preparation had meant a lack of blisters or bad feet, and energy levels were holding up well. Even Susie Burton whose slight frame and minimal diet made me wonder if she had the stamina for this venture, never faltered, and my impression was that if asked, our troubadours could have carried on walking and performing into the autumn and beyond. Next tour the Great Wall of China?

We were to be filmed for the second time by a television crew. The alarmingly tall Jonathan Hill and his cameraman Jonathan Reed from Tyne-Tees Television (who obviously had a bigger budget than Border TV) had arranged to meet us *en route* and they tracked us down

East of Chollerford at a place called Planetrees. It was at Planetrees that the writer William Hutton had chastised locals for nicking off with stone from the ancient monument (an illustration of the same chastisement is on the cover of Hutton's book in the Frank Graham 1990 reprint), and I assumed that the large and impressive farmhouse close by had been the result of such theft. As far as I knew no-one had counted up the number of houses, churches, pig sties, village halls and pubs that had been built from the Roman Wall along its length but it was obviously considerable, and this theft had seemed no big deal until Hutton had come along and wagged his finger at such practice. After this, public opinion shifted, and preserving the wall became accepted behaviour, Try to nick off with any stone now, and about eighteen different Roman Wall authorities and organisations will be down on you like a ton of — well, stone.

The TV crew shot us at Planetrees, they shot us walking past the distinctive church of Heavensfield (said to be full of spirits, and the site of a famous battle), and they shot us sitting outside the delightful St. Oswald tea rooms which almost marks the summit after the long steep haul out of Chollerford. You can get a big hot mug of chocolate here for £1.05p and many of us did.

If you'd been involved with television in any way (and I'd dipped in and out over the years) you got used to the enthusiasm TV people generated towards their subject of the time, an enthusiasm that made the object of their attention feel pretty important. Later you realised this enthusiasm was mainly manufactured, part of the behaviour pattern and could be turned on and off like a tap, so that a few weeks down the line the same crew would probably be hard put to remember you at all. Working in television was seen as glamorous, and half the young people in the country aspired to it. It fed the ego too, and for actors it was obviously the place to be but I'd found TV work often a shallow unfulfilling experience, and it held few attractions for me.

Having said which, Jonathan Hill proved to be a man of some integrity. His enthusiasm towards the play stretched as far as saying he'd like to come and see it, an intention I half-dismissed as more ersatz zeal, but a few nights later, in one of the post-Wall Tyneside performances, there he was, his tall figure striding in the door and waving, and my cynicism was put firmly in its place.

In the TV interview I wanted Jonathan to ask me searching questions about the play's structure, style and social relevance; but this interview was for the early evening mass audience news, so quite understandably the questions concerned the pursuit by the bull, Dylan's Olympic dive, and how he and Bill E. Meeks had ended up in hospital, the latter on a saline drip.

I had this growing impression of the Roman Wall, that it held in some distaste the development of humankind, so that where society had developed into large industrialised conurbations, the wall hid itself away, refused to show, and only in the wilder countryside, the areas where it still felt at home, did Hadrian's Wall rise up in all its magnificence and breathe freely.

Now that the countryside was beginning to flatten out and civilisation grew closer, the wall was retreating into its shell. Its regular invisibility hereabouts was also due to General Wade's vandalism in building the military road directly on the wall's top, and where there *was* evidence of the wall, it was not the great beast striding out across the countryside, but something more sad and confined. At Planetrees the stretch of wall was enclosed inside a fence, and it felt like some wild animal locked up in a zoo.

We trudged on. The path criss-crossed the Military Road several times, and we now had little more than the vallum to remind us of the wall's once existence. Which was OK, but how many people get excited about a ditch? So that the walk was in some ways an act of faith, especially if you were heading east to west, (which we weren't.) Imagine you had travelled from somewhere abroad to walk the wall's entire 84 miles. If you'd left Segedunum (Wallsend) you'd already have been tramping for three days with little more to see than the odd brown cow.

We stopped for lunch at the Errington Arms, situated by the Postgate roundabout on the A68. Travel along this road if you like the excitement of switchback riding. It's straight but plunges and soars in short bursts and offers warning signs such as SEVERE DIP.

The Errington, named after a local landowning family, is a pleasant large stone building in a prominent position. We sat at one of the outside tables and arranged our coloured flags in jousting tournament formation on the lawn for the benefit of passing motorists. We took out our packed lunches, and I felt so guilty I went inside to the bar to buy a soft drink I didn't want. No-one else bothered.

Joining us for lunch was our stage manager Craig. Craig was our contact with the normal world beyond the confines of this wall. We seven were on this trajectory, this 84 miles odyssey that daily took us further along the length of this ancient monument. We never varied from our path; we wandered hardly a single yard from our prescribed route. Ours was a tunnel vision and a narrow tunnel at that.

But Craig's daily route was quite different. Though he was also "locked into" the wall in many ways, he had to whiz hither and thither on our behalf. He had to replace broken flags, do the washing, pick up extra waterproofs, provide a new keyboard or whatever other contingency arose that day. Craig reminded me of those people in the game of curling who frantically brush the ice to ensure the stones have an easy progress. That was Craig, assuring at all times that the way ahead was smooth, that we would not be distracted from our task, which was to complete the day's walk and perform the play in the evening.

We were met on the road that afternoon by my partner, the writer Kitty Fitzgerald. Her new novel had that very day been bought for a considerable sum by Faber & Faber, and as she walked towards us, we broke out singing its title, *Pigtopia*, to the tune of *Jerusalem,* which may have meant we sounded like some itinerant branch of the WI.

Kitty's good fortune meant she would, for the first time in her life, soon have cash in the bank. I had no idea how she would handle this, neither I suspect, did she.

This was probably our most event-free day. We arrived at the Robin Hood well in time, to be told there was another sell-out audience. The Robin Hood is a well-known landmark in the North-East, a beautiful old pub with a restaurant extension at the rear, and big ambitions. These included the aforesaid (but doomed not to be erected) permanent marquee which would have had regular discos. Several locals had objected including our landlady for the night, Brenda Walton who ran The Barn, the B & B right next to the pub.

This may have explained why, when we asked Brenda if she were coming to the show, she answered with a shake of the head and the reply, "I'll be sitting with my feet up." It brought home how what might look like a rural idyll could often be dreadfully claustrophobic. Small tight communities were often more fractious than anonymous urban ones, where at least the ripples of disagreement could melt away into the same anonymity. Brenda Walton only had one set of neighbours. And she was in dispute with them.

We ate early in the restaurant, which offered fresh tuna steaks to die for. Actors didn't like to eat too near a performance. It made them sluggish, and also an attack of nerves was less likely to produce vomiting if the food was already well digested.

Once again I employed my revolutionary lo-tech method of getting the article to *The Journal*. I can't even begin to describe the job satisfaction such an old-fashioned method gave me.

I felt sorry for Steve Chettle. He'd not only sorted out the hiring and erecting of the performance tent, but he'd hired and erected a second smaller marquee for the actors to use as changing rooms. Only in the latter stages of erecting this (which was no mean feat) did he realise one side was totally open and it was this side that faced out along the path the audience walked, so that it would be like getting changed in a shop window. Thus this tent stood unused like some strange canvas folly. We changed at the B & B.

The weather had set in badly. From 6pm a steady rain fell, the cloud was grey, unbroken and low, and the temperatures had dropped considerably. The ground had already been soggy and was now more so. We'd hired a large amount of matting to cover the floor inside the marquee, but the sensation was rather like walking on a water bed, except a water bed did not leak. As you applied your foot to this matting, it sank beneath you and water oozed up round the sides of your shoe.

And although the Robin Hood itself was fairly isolated, the nearby Military Road, being straight and fast and directly east-west, attracted a fair bit of traffic which hurtled past at high decibel count. Add to this the delights of low-flying military aircraft which the RAF employed regularly and you'll realise our performance would have more than its fair share of distractions.

Setting up the lights proved problematic too. The soggy surface meant it was almost impossible for Craig to properly stabilise them, and hence accurate focussing became difficult. The temperature inside the tent was a bit higher than outside, but hardly enough bring anyone out into a sweat.

When I introduced the show, the cast would be hanging around outside the door and at a given signal, made their big entrance. They always assembled there well in time, which meant a bit of waiting around. Normally it was no problem, but on this night waiting outside the door meant waiting in the rain and the wind. The idea on the big entrance was for the cast to look as if they'd just that minute finished a day's walking along the wall. At the Robin Hood tent the illusion was perfect. They looked a bit like drowned rats. It was not the ideal starting point for a play.

The cast were cold, the audience were cold, and what had seemed a fairly undemanding day thus far, now became an evening's performance of considerable challenge.

Everyone — cast, audience, technicians, and writer needed a warm infusion. Hot toddies all round would have been ace. This wasn't possible. Plus which the lack of black-out meant the lights struggled to make an effect, and hence the atmosphere was diluted. And just for good measure, did I notice a few of the seats going wonky on the waterlogged ground?

The show opened again with Ruth Lambert and Sarah Rickard doing the same three North-East numbers, against an impressionistic backdrop, one of three produced in workshops with the artist Richard Jardine, with the intriguing graffiti-style words DAWALL.

It was a struggle for the singers. But sometimes the worst brings out the best. Thus it was here. A kind of bloody mindedness slowly set in, the attitude tabloids love to call The Dunkirk Spirit, a determination to succeed in spite of circumstance. I felt it in the cast, and in the audience who had braved the elements to sit in the cold and damp in their big coats to see our show. I had no idea where most of this audience hailed from, this being an isolated venue, but they deserved medals.

For the opening ten minutes people were more aware of their damp feet than the brilliant verbal interplay between characters. But then the show began to pick up pace. The turning point was the song, *Everything is for Sale*. I'm not overkeen on songs in theatre and would travel across mountains and wild oceans to miss the artificiality of most musicals. But I was grateful for the power of music and singing to lift an excessively damp audience. So maybe that song *was* our hot toddy.

It was also heartening to spot not a single spare seat. A week previously The Robin Hood had informed us they'd sold only one ticket, and I was moodily concluding that such an isolated venue, unattached to a village, would fail to bring them flocking in. But bring them in it did.

So that as the performance progressed, my thoughts became more positive. One of my life's delights — possibly more than rhubarb crumble and sometimes not far behind sex — was in witnessing a live audience connecting with what I'd written and what was taking place up on that stage. This was an experience denied to writers for TV and radio, that almost tangible sense that the audience were picking up on the conflicts, struggle and issues, the comedy or the tragedy that had been fought hard and long for by the writer. And the fact that a radio or TV audience may number millions counted for little when you couldn't see them. A theatre audience was like a shared heartbeat when the play was working, something a playwright knew instinctively. Just as he/she instinctively knew the opposite, when the words were falling flatter than a fart, but let's not go into that right now.

So that here in this draughty isolated marquee on a cold and miserable Northumberland night, the elements eventually became secondary, and the play was the thing. I was a peripatetic audience member as usual during my own plays; I walked about, took up different positions and angles. I wanted to know how these people reacted to the rapacious entrepreneur Loot (Dave Hollingworth). What were their feelings and emotions about his lonely if feisty wife, Dolores (Janine Birkett)? What about Bill E. Meeks as Loot's side-kick Cogno, who obviously knew much more than he let on? Would the audience take to him or mistrust him? Or Alex Kinsey's Blairite politician and the same actor's camp Roman Governor of Britain? Or Susie Burton's blond gold-digger, or Dylan Mortimer's Caledonian rebel?

Unlike real life, a play allowed the onlooker the luxury of uninterrupted study of their subject. We could sit undisturbed for around one hour observing and drawing conclusions about the people up there on stage. Staring at these people was not considered impolite. Indeed it was obligatory. And our views were not compromised; these characters, because they did not exist, could be of no "use" to us in real life. We did not have to curry favour with them. Nor were we prejudiced against them for the kind of historical reason that often left family members not talking to one another over decades. Thus our reactions, give or take the odd human foible, were fairly uncorrupted and in that area at least a play could be more real than reality (discuss).

By now I could recite the play line-by-line. But, as any play should, it kept throwing up surprises for me. Lines I had never thought of as humorous produced hoots of laughter. Where I'd convinced myself I'd created the funniest scene since Laurel & Hardy, the audience might sit in stony silence.

Despite the primitive conditions, I took to the idea of theatre in a tent. In the 1950s the great Irish impresario Tyrone Guthrie had toured plays in a large marquee, and I wanted to do it too.

Whenever a circus came to the grassed area on the sea front close to where I live, called Beaconsfield, I was excited to see the great tent go up, and the small community encamped around it always stirred something romantic in me.

I wanted to stir people's blood with a theatre tent. And give them an experience they'd never previously had.

Meantime, we were two days from home.

***

Sometimes a writer is hard put to think up anything which is outrageous enough *not* to risk coming true. One ambition of my play was to satirise the UK's contemporary market-driven culture via the device of an entrepreneur turning the Roman Wall into the world's longest theme park. Thus I let my imagination rip when writing these scenes. Loot's scheme transforms the wall's wild splendour so that visitors travel via a mono-rail encased in plastic, mile castles become fast food outlets where customers are gleefully urged to "have a nice day!", out-of-work actors engage in mock centurion battles at designated places. And customers can engage in Play Station style computer games at regular intervals.

Later that night in the bar of the Robin Hood, as the audience and cast thawed out a man came up to engage me in conversation.

"A pretty good concept that you had for the wall there," he said and I was looking for the irony or send-up in the voice, but there was none. He later announced himself as Miles Middleton, the chair of the Hadrian Wall Tourism Partnership.

Brenda Walton of our night's residence The Barn, enquired later about our physical state. "A lot of people don't understand what walking the whole wall entails," she said, "a lot of them aren't up to it."

"Some of them who set off from the east give up by the time they get here. They've trudged 21 miles and seen virtually nothing."

Twenty-one miles. After a couple of drinks, as the pub began to empty I walked out into the silence and dark of the military road at 11.30pm. If I looked west whence where we had already travelled, the sky was inky black and unpolluted. I was staring back at the play's history. Look to the east, and the play's short future, and the sky was streaked with the orange light that announced the pending arrival of the Tyneside conurbation. Day by day we were being sucked back to the inevitable.

And the journey was having some effect. Jan Birkett, whose high energy singing carried most of the songs, was worried about her voice at low register. Dylan's foot was still a bit wonky. And being on the road day after day we were finding that much of our luggage was beginning to fall to bits. Which was preferable to the same fate being visited on ourselves.

Chapter Nine

Mr Chettle Under Suspicion, and Blowing the System

This was our penultimate day. Accommodation at the Barn that night had been limited, so two of us had to take B& B at the nearby hamlet of Harlow Hill. Harlow Hill was east along the Military Road which meant one of my unwritten rules was broken. This rule stated none of us should venture further along our route at any time other than by walking it with the rest of the troupe. The walk had to be, as it were, "virgin."

Necessity — ie lack of accommodation near the Robin Hood — meant the rule had to be disobeyed. I suspected no-one else apart from me was that worried.

To compensate for my deep distress, the two — Bill Meeks and Alex Kinsey — were whisked back to the Robin Hood start point to set off on that day's ten mile journey to Throckley.

Throckley was part of the great Newcastle conurbation, lying on the city's outer western fringe. This was to be the first urban performance, and we had no idea how an audience might respond. Throckley was not the most glamorous of areas and our Throckley Hall had an unprepossessing appearance which had caused it to slink off and hide down a back lane.

We'd grown accustomed to the remote and the rural. We normal urbanites had adapted to a new normality these last seven days. We now took as natural striding out over wind-swept ledges against panoramic spectacular depopulated backdrops. We would be returning to the land of double yellow lines, neighbourhood watch, the jangling of ignored burglar alarms. We would be back to disaffected yoof, urban blight, traffic jams, and littered streets.

This knowledge of what awaited us on this and the next day — the long trudge across almost the entire conurbation of Newcastle and North Tyneside — made us more appreciative than normal of the trees field and hedges our journey still had to offer. Our route was now virtually flat and we were rarely more than a few yards from the road which the Roman trail criss-crossed regularly.

One compensation was that an increasing number of motorists were hooting us and waving to us. We took this to be friendly.

The wall itself was now mainly becoming memory. In fact we were walking on top of the wall, which was buried beneath the road. On each side of us the great Tyne Valley folded back its hills like opening wings, and on these hills the houses gathered in increasing numbers.

Throughout our days' walks, spotting Steve Chettle had become a popular sport for all of us. Steve was making a photographic and video documentation of our journey and performances. He applied himself to this task with such dedication, and from so many different positions that we would not have been surprised to see him hanging from some fluffy cloud, snapping us from above. We would spot Steve, tripod in position perched on top of a giddy peak, at the end of a long stretch of road, or up at the far end of a distant field. There was a certain kudos for being the first to spot Steve.

Steve's dedication had produced some great photographs, especially in the wall's wildest areas. My favourite was a long distance shot, all seven of us, with bright fluttering flags silhouetted on top of a high and lonely ridge. This photograph seemed to say something special about our strange odyssey.

But Steve's photographic zeal was about to land him in trouble. We all know that Britain has more CCTV cameras than any country in the world; that it has become a land where it's impossible to pick your nose without it being documented on film. The authorities have *carte blanche* to spy on us whenever and wherever they see fit, but the reverse it appears is not true. They don't like being spied on in return. Nor did we expect high security right out here in rural England. Or maybe the British Army was just following the 2000 year old tradition about this being a military frontier, and was acting out of historical necessity.

Steve had set up his tripod this morning on a long straight stretch of road not far from Albermarle army barracks, and he took a series of photos as we trudged towards him.

He'd been snapping away only a few moments (and not once was the camera trained on the barracks which lay off the main road) when an Army Land Rover appeared, out jumped two members of Her Majesty's armed forces, and Mr Chettle was interrogated.

Clearly it had to be established if this were an al Qaeda threat. Doubts had to be satisfied that a small travelling theatre company walking the Roman Wall did not constitute a national security hazard. Mr Chettle, post-questioning, was allowed to continue on his way. But no doubt somewhere his name will be on file. The army's interests in our activities by the way did not stretch to coming to see a performance.

Our brightly coloured flags had proved remarkably resilient on the journey, despite often extreme weather. There were adorned with the odd squashed fly or splat of mud, yet were still as defiantly vivid as when we set off from Bowness-on-Solway (which now seemed a distant memory). Their long poles often proved impractical, and were given to snagging on overhead branches, yanking us back like recalcitrant school children pulled up by teacher. But I loved to see us gathered in unison, bright flags to the fore. If asked I'd have scoffed at the idea of uniforms, denounced them as controlling and conforming devices, be it in schools, the army or anywhere else, but what were these flags if not our uniform?

Among souvenirs gathered en route was a series of commonplace flowers which Susie and Janine had pressed between the pages of a book. For some reason this was an activity which would rarely have entered the heads of most males. "Girlie stuff," said Susie in a deliberately self-deprecatory fashion.

Tyneside from the west begins with Heddon-on-the-Wall, part rural, part urban, and offering the last substantial evidence of Hadrian's Wall itself. From hereon in there's little to be seen of this great monument; you might spot the miniscule example on a garage forecourt which dogs peed on, but which was ignored by the rest of the world, and the odd lump was fenced in here and there, but you'd need a keen eye.

The example at Heddon was substantial, several hundred yards long and just off the main road. I had been there several times, and had yet to see another visitor. It was on this stretch I'd stood to pose for the ill-advised newspaper photograph that had metaphorically seen me tarred and feathered by the wall authorities.

We pitched our midday camp in the Heddon rest garden, arranged our flags in formation on the grass, and took the quick walk to the Dingly Dell eatery for tea and coffee. We were cheered up when the counter assistant said she'd been following the articles every day in *The Journal*, but we were slightly deflated by the two Roman Wall wardens who were sat eating scones, and said they hadn't a clue who any of us were.

From Heddon onwards we would be back-in-touch with the reality that is much of modern-day urban Britain; drab buildings, hooting traffic, cheap supermarkets, tatty bus stops, steel-shuttered shops, disconsolate yoof gathered on corners. En route to our night's accommodation, we called at the somewhat undistinguished Throckley Community

Hall; where we were due to perform. Craig was already setting up lights and sound and set. From here we headed down the hill towards the river and our night's destination, The Keelman at Newburn.

Now those of you suspecting we were again breaking my rule of not journeying the next day's route ahead of time, be assured our next day's route from The Keelman was different from the one we were travelling today.

Like Throckley, Newburn was not among Newcastle's fashionable areas. It lies on the edge of the city's huge sprawling West End, which takes in Benwell, Elswick and Blaydon, none of which had traditionally been much sought after. Much of the region had been neglected, and become devastated and vandalised, so that some houses had been put up for sale at 50p (and often not taken up), while in other areas of the city people would spend half a million to get a dog kennel. Great swathes of industry had been destroyed along the riverside. Jerry flats had been shoved up and then pulled down. Newcastle Council still had plans to raze whole areas to the ground but had met much resistance from a local populace who fought against such instant obliteration of memory, and the situation was still in a state of flux.

This had once probably been the most industrialised stretch of river anywhere in the world, yet the only real remaining heavyweight evidence of that industrialisation was the Vickers tank factory. The legendary and quixotic Tyneside politician T. Dan Smith had left his legacy here in the 60s and 70s, but this legacy too had mainly passed away.

Much of Tyneside had become high-profile in recent years, with the remarkable renaissance of the once derelict Quayside — the Sage Music Centre, the Millennium Bridge, the Baltic Arts Centre (all it must be said on the Southern Gateshead side of the river). The Quayside was now an exhilarating place to be, but less exhilarating, and much less in the public spotlight were the great western stretches of the city. These was so poor, and so neglected that when in the early 80s the Metro rapid transit system had been built (the first, and as it transpired, probably the last to be built in the country), the west end of Newcastle, despite its large population had been totally ignored, while areas such as Jesmond and Gosforth (where people who decided such things lived) were generously endowed with stations.

As we dropped down towards the river, I could sense our spirits dropping too. There was a sense of anti-climax about this. We wanted our adventure to end in a blaze of glory but it seemed we were being sucked into the great amorphous anonymity of a city, to be swallowed up without comment or notice. The city was beginning to press in on us, and perhaps it would render us invisible, or simply cage us. And where we had stridden through the open countryside without inhibition, now I felt slightly cowed, aware we were being stared at, and not always certain the stares were of a friendly nature.

So it was with a sense of welcome surprise that we walked into the grounds of The Keelman. This was a converted stone pumping station that also housed the Big Lamp, one of the splendid micro-breweries that against all the odds had taken on the big conglomerates over recent years and more than held their own.

The Keelman was surrounded by leafy tree-lined gardens in which family groups were gathered round wooden tables enjoying the late afternoon sunshine. It was close to the river and seemed to have pushed back the more depressing aspects of the encroaching city. Plus which, as we walked up the drive and to the main entrance, some of these garden folk actually broke into applause. Nobody had done this for us except on stage.

And on this day we had walked 9.5 miles, taken 19,950 steps and used up 680 calories — not bad statistics for an average person's exertion, but low for we superfit luvvies.

We ate at The Keelman in a large glass extension that made you feel like a tropical plant at Kew Gardens. By now there was little need to be given stage notes, nor for director Jackie Fielding to say very much to the actors. They were a perfectly co-ordinated team. I felt they could perform *Off the Wall* on top of Everest if required. It had become second nature to them. I had fewer nerves at a performance than in any of the previous 17 plays I had written. What could go wrong now?

Quite a bit actually, as Throckley was to prove.

Our accommodation was an annexe, clean, modern, well-appointed if anonymous rooms. One of the pleasures of each day was stretching out on a bed at journey's end, that relaxing sense of self-congratulation that one more destination had been reached. This indulgence was short lived; for the actors because they had to mentally prepare for performance; for me, because I had to pen, and transmit, those 800 words to *The Journal*.

And if I were something of a technophobe, Steve Chettle was a technophile. He was a abreast of all modern computer technology and could quite happily discuss the likes of blue tooth, wired keyboards, SuperDrive options or other phrases that produced in me a look of glazed incomprehension. He was proud of his ARTS UK set-up and rightly so, and it lay less than half a mile from The Keelman.

He was keen for me to file that night's copy via his own computer set-up. This produced mixed feelings in me. I knew I would be in safe hands, and that any glitches would be sorted. The copy would get through via hi-technology. But I also thought of my unseen copy-taker friend Sandy sitting, no doubt in his windowless room, headphones at the ready. Sandy and I had re-established our long moribund relationship these past days, and though little was said between us (we were men, see?) I sensed it had a strange importance for him, just as it did for me.

Enough sentimentality. The article was written, and sent incident-free — plus that day's photographs. Time was a newspaper such as *The Journal* would despatch a photographer each day to chronicle such a journey. Now we were expected to take our own pics, send them down the wire, and not a penny in payment. We did it because it needed to be done, but what did professional photographers think to see our own, often far from perfect efforts splashed across the pages? Nor, nowadays did the union have much to say in the matter. Like many unions, the NUJ had become an enfeebled beast.

No two live performances were ever the same. This was a cliché, but an important one, and it was reinforced at Throckley Hall when, twenty minutes before we were due to go up, our electrical system blew, leaving us with no lights.

"Hmm," said stage manager Craig. Craig was one of those unflappable people who might manifest slight distress if being eaten alive by Godzilla, but nothing too panicky. For over-excitable people such as me, the Craigs of this world were vital for survival.

He set to on repairs, with the short phrase, "keep your fingers crossed." I didn't have to. I had this total belief Craig would fix it. Which he did. Five minutes before we went up, one of Dylan's guitar strings snapped. Luckily we carried spares. And then there was the member of the audience, an elderly man who half an hour into the show, stood up from the main body of seats, plonked himself down in a chair at the rear of the hall and within five minutes was snoring loudly, an unexpected sound effect.

There was also the small matter of Dave Hollingworth's tattoo. Or in this case non-tattoo. He and Alex would felt-tip in the Celtic design on Dave's back each night, in readiness for the scene proving that the modern entrepreneur Loot has been transformed into a Caledonian chieftain. At Throckley they forgot, and for a second time an audience had unadorned skin to stare at.

The Hall was one of those fairly basic, but cosy centres that somehow survive in modern Britain. We had an audience of eighty, mainly of the somewhat advanced age of people who kept community centres going. There was a solidity and steadfastness about them, they sold tea for 20p a cup, and there was a raffle. Indeed the cast had barely delivered the play's last line than a white-haired lady jumped up at the front of the audience. I thought she was going to thank Cloud Nine for coming to put on such a splendid performance, but she shouted out "number one hundred and forty six!" which was the winning ticket. She said nothing else and left the stage.

Our musician that night was again the Northumbrian piper Sue Dunn, and the backdrop had been created with local people working alongside artist Richard Jardine.

Throckley Community Hall was a down-to-earth, no-nonsense place. Did I sense a slight disapproval, just a hint that it was time the likes of us got proper jobs and stopped messing on? I couldn't quite put my finger on this. Maybe it was the proximity to the sites of heavy industry on which Tyneside's previous prosperity had been built, and because those who worked in a sweltering steel mill all day probably had little respect for the "hard" work of an actor.

Maybe it was due to the Protestant work ethic, which could still have a hold on me, and which implied that if you enjoyed your work, it wasn't real work and you weren't a real person. I knew this was absurd, and that we should concentrate our efforts into making work pleasurable for more, not fewer people, and that the dignity of labour meant very little if that labour were either physically or mentally soul-destroying.

But the guilt still lingered somewhere in the dark recesses — that you got paid for work mainly because there would be no way you'd do it otherwise. Whereas a writer had no option. If they were genuine, they *had* to write, and just hope they were lucky enough to be given some cash. It was an easily exploited instinct, so that for some unfortunates it wasn't simply a case of not being paid, but actually paying to do it. Just look at the number of unsuspecting writers persuaded to cough up huge sums for publication in the dingy area of vanity publishing. Can you imagine plumbers ever paying a load of dosh for the luxury of replacing u-bends?

And after the play, drinks in the balmy garden of The Keelman, and a certain melancholy in the camp, the knowledge that come the next and final day, all this would melt away, the close bonding we had known would simply dissolve, we would go our separate ways and whatever the heartfelt assurances to "keep in touch', most of simply wouldn't.

Chapter Ten

Now we are Eight — and a Latin Welcome

Our final day would see a trudge across Tyneside, into the heart of Newcastle, then out again towards Wallsend and Segedunum, where the whole journey had started that cold and blustery morning ten days (or was it two millennia?) ago.

Certain things on our journey had been impossible to find. Alex Kinsey had searched in vain for a cash machine (I found this hi-tech gap rather comforting). My son Dylan had looked long and hard in the hope of a milk shake. Some things we had found an excess of. I was tiring of sandwiches, and could happily go the rest of my life without seeing or tasting a grated cheese sandwich in particular. Who invented this habit of grating rather than slicing cheese for a sandwich? Most of the cheese ended up on the floor (or in our case the grass), and there was nothing to bite on. Also, plodging about in muddy fields had come to lack any appeal after the last few days, and large rampant bulls had little fascination for me now.

We decided to head off early this day, with up to fourteen miles to cover. We were up so early in our annexe, the milk was still on the step of The Keelman proper when we went over for breakfast.

This would be the last time in the history of the universe that this exact group of people would sit down together for breakfast. The thought was a depressing one, but not enough to put me off my egg, bacon and sausage.

Although the day's walking was lengthy, on the positive side we would be hugging the river all day which meant no gradients, nor indeed any rough surfaces. It would be impossible to get lost.

Much of our route was on reclaimed ground. Where once these river banks had been scarred with belching factories, now the likes of Elswick and Scotswood offered riverside walks, and installation sculptures. The mud flats were still pretty unsavoury. Vickers long pencil of a factory still belched and roared, and the remains of Dunston Staithes (which had been set on fire in 2003) reminded you of the time the "coaly Tyne" once shipped 140,000 tons of coal every week. We were now walking through a much different, much more recent history than we'd been exposed to these last nine days.

And one thing I knew. Nothing here would survive anything like the duration of the Roman Wall. These offices, shops, factories, schools, libraries — in two millennia they would not even be memory. In fact it was unthinkable that anything manufactured or constructed in 2005 would still be around in 4005. Yet the wall was still with us.

We had no sooner left The Keelman than from out of nowhere popped a small man in khaki walking shorts, sturdy boots, thick socks, a haversack, and a peaked cap. There was something slightly comic about this figure, something that reminded me of the *Carry On* films. A touch of the Kenneth Connor with maybe a hint of Charles Hautrey. He announced himself as Malcolm McVey, a keen walker from Rowlands Gill. He said that he had been in the previous night's audience and had decided to walk with us all day. The next minute he was striding out by our side and would continue to be there for several hours. At one stage he disappeared as mysteriously as he had arrived but then reappeared, again just as mysteriously.

I didn't know the man personally but the sense of we brave few walking in triumph through Tyneside together had long been in my mind. Jan Birkett said it didn't matter and he was only being friendly, and she was probably right, but I felt especially protective about our group. I said none of this to Malcolm, though I did carefully guide him out of shot when we took photographs along Newcastle Quayside with the Tyne Bridge behind us. This was not to be documented as the Magnificent Eight.

He walked all the way to Segedunum. When we stopped for a rest Malcolm stopped for a rest. When we set off again, he set off again. He chatted on quite a bit and some of us chatted back easily and some others didn't. At Segedunum he turned on his heel, said "thank you very much" and started walking back, presumably to Rowlands Gill, and that was the end (for us) of Malcolm McVey.

Our journey took us though the tough area of Scotswood, where a group of chavers cycled past and yelled "freaks!" I realised this probably wasn't a bad description for a group of seven people walking into a city centre with bright flags protruding from their backs. Before long we were progressing along Newcastle's much vaunted and renovated quayside busy with its Saturday shoppers, strollers, drinkers and diners. Several people looked at us strangely but none asked us who we were, so that simultaneously urban folk seemed more aggressive yet less curious than those in the countryside. A three headed alien could probably have walked here without any questions.

Like most big cities, Newcastle had "discovered" its river in the previous decade, reversing the quayside decline which had begun in the 30s with the building of the Tyne Bridge. This new bridge had meant traffic no longer needed to drop down to the riverside to cross the water, and thus the area became neglected. Now the riverside was full of bars, restaurants and posh apartments, though on a global scale it had attracted attention through that trio of breathtaking new ventures, the Baltic, the Sage Music Centre, and the Millennium Bridge. Newcastle had been responsible for none of these. Nor did it house them. Its previous Cinderella South-side neighbour Gateshead had created all three, for which it never received due credit.

Newcastle and Gateshead were now joined by seven bridges, two of which moved about, the Millennium Bridge ("The Blinking Eye") and the 1876 swing bridge which moved through 90 degrees to allow passage for the occasional large vessel.

Today's rest periods were somewhat different. In the morning we sat outside the plush Copthorne Hotel and ate our sandwiches. And later on we took a rest outside a trendy waterside bistro at St. Peters Basin, one of the riverside's first yuppie developments with its own marina. The wild stretches of the Roman Wall seemed far distant.

And on towards Wallsend, with its dramatic ship building cranes, which rose up into the sky like giant predatory insects. We finally left the river and wended our way up through a seemingly endless succession of tarmac paths and walkways towards Segedunum, and its 34 metre high tower, a giant eye on a stalk from some sci-fi movie.

This is the wall's end or beginning (though no-one presumably thought of calling the town Wallstart), and an important archaeological site. That said, it's as flat as a snooker table and at first glance of little interest. Up in the observation tower you can create computer models of how it would have looked nearly two millennia ago, and relate it to the actual site below. For more physical evidence, the reconstructed bath house offer rows of open toilets which conjure images of a line of defecating Romans.

There was a sense of anti-climax at reaching our destination. Had we expected a brass band, bright bunting, the local Mayor in all his regalia with outstretched hand?

We trudged the last few yards under a sullen sky, a group of seven tired looking individuals with coloured flags. Though our arrival was not without some ceremony. One of Cloud Nine's writers, Noreen Rees welcomed us with a specially made banner which read *Saluto Victori Fortissimus*, translated as *Welcome the Conquering*

Heroes, and I felt quite touched, despite feeling neither heroic nor conquering.

Steve Chettle had booked rooms in the only nearby hotel The Hadrian's Lodge to allow us to prepare for that night's performance at Segedunum itself. The hotel was three quarters of a mile away in the kind of blighted urban landscape that made you want to whistle a Leonard Cohen song.

The idea was for two taxis to take us there, but only one showed up and three of us were left to trudge the dismal route to the hotel. This wasn't physically demanding, being less than a mile. Mentally it took some effort, firstly because Segedunum should have been journey's end walk-wise, secondly because the landscape of ugly factories, waste land and drab development dragged down the human spirit.

Nor was this mood helped when we arrived to find all our luggage had been deposited back at Segedunum itself, and, for some reason, up on the third floor. Nor did we take much comfort from the featureless nature of the hotel. The outside sign had obviously once displayed two AA stars, but it had been demoted and one had been painted out. I suspected the second was also in danger. There were only two rooms between seven of us. One room stunk of stale cigarette smoke, and was almost entirely filled with a double bed, leaving no floor space.

I went to reception and booked a third room. We then needed to fetch our luggage from Segedunum. Jan Birkett decided to flee back to her own home (which was in Wallsend), and I shared her taxi, dropping off back to Segedunum, where Craig was setting up for the show. He and I carried seven people's luggage downstairs, and into the company van which I then drove back to the hotel. I wasn't insured, but quite frankly at that moment I didn't give a toss.

I think, ironically, here at journey's end where we should have felt some sense of achievement, our spirits were lower than at any time on the journey. They revived slightly when after freshening up, we ate in the dining room and the food wasn't as quite bad as we'd expected. The bar was sprinkled with young Wallsend bloods on the early stages of a Saturday night's bladdering. There was also a slight upwards lift when we heard the night's performance was sold out, and they could have flogged the tickets three times over.

But we all wanted shut of the hotel. At 6pm, we loaded up the van and I drove it one more time, and again illegally, the short journey to Segedunum. I sensed the dismal cloud lifting slightly, and of course the adrenalin of a live performance to come always set in about this time.

Our performance area at Segedunum was small. They'd crammed in fifty seats but the front row was close enough to the actors for the audience to risk being poked in the eye by our flags. And with such proximity you wouldn't want either audience or cast to be suffering from halitosis.

The singer that night was called Roger Oram. He was employed at Segedunum, and he sang unaccompanied, and the backdrop had again been made in workshops with Richard Jardine. Our audience seemed pretty knowledgeable about the wall and its history. Throughout the tour I'd been expecting some wall expert or other (and there were plenty of the species on the ground) to pick me up on some errant detail. I'd done a fair bit of research, read books, articles, travelled the length of the wall twice, spoken to academics, yet compared to the wall zealots and experts, I was a tyro. I had picked up some odd facts in my work and as a bit of fun had included in the programme a page headed *Ten Things You Never Knew About the Roman Wall*, including the plan to rebuild the wall at a cost of £30,000 in the Elizabethan era when they were worried (as ever) about those marauding Scots. But generally, the more I learnt about Hadrian's Wall, the more it emphasised how little I knew.

And though visual evidence of the wall had been slight the last two days, here at Segedunum we were steeped in its history, the display of artefacts, the reconstructed buildings, the books, the posters.

We had traversed the wall's length, and performed along its entirety. As far as I knew, we had done what no other theatre company had done, walking and performing the width of England a play along the wall, about the wall, for people who lived close to the wall.

Interest in, and demand for the play had grown as our journey progressed, so that although our walking was done, we'd been booked to do two extra performances, one at The Magnesia Bank pub in North Shields, the second across the water at Arbeia Roman Fort in South Shields.

Yet this brace of performances would not be quite the same. We would not be walking to our destination. We would not, as a band of troubadours, be striding away the next morning. Neither would have a specially created banner. Our great wall adventure, in the true sense would end here at Segedunum.

Just as we'd made a journey, so too had the play, evolving as we travelled. I thought I'd written a rapacious entrepreneur in the character Loot, but Dave Hollingworth came to discover a vulnerable and sympathetic side too. I thought Loot's wife Dolores was a put-upon woman, but Jan Birkett's interpretation also produced a great feistiness. Bill E. Meek's manservant Cogno became simultaneously a working class lad struggling to survive, and a subtle manipulator of his master. Alex Kinsey managed to make the Roman governor of Britain both effete and ruthless, while Dylan Mortimer's Caledonian tribesman was both fiercely patriotic and hugely comic. Susie Burton's bimbo I saw as a fairly empty-headed gold-digger, but you ended up feeling quite sorry for her. All of which proved you were never quite sure of the characters you created, and — quite rightly — they demanded a life of their own.

Would the actors' interpretation had been the same if this had been a conventional production, and they'd simply turned up at the same theatre nine nights running?

Had the journey itself affected what happened on stage? We would never know.

Thus the sun went down on our Roman Wall tour for the final time. There were no hitches in the performance and the response from the tightly packed audience was enthusiastic. We ourselves were somewhat melancholic. We took down the set, the cast got changed. Somehow no-one wanted a big party. In the dressing room our director Jackie Fielding opened a bottle of warmish champagne which we sipped from paper cups, People exchanged gifts. It was the end but not the end. It was a hiatus, and we weren't sure how to respond. The next morning we would wake up in our own beds, and have no journey. Yet two performances still lay ahead.

For the first time, there was no visit to the pub. We had arrived and performed in a succession of tiny communities. It was a journey that had touched our lives significantly and we hoped, the lives of some others. We had been washed away, pursued by bulls, hospitalised. On some days we had been so exhausted we could barely speak, but the actors had always recovered the energy levels in time for the performance. The whole venture had possibly more in spirit with the 1960s than the more utilitarian start to the 21st century, but if so, what the heck? Somehow we'd got the funding, and we'd gone and done it. And I had known deep down, even when the obstacles seemed major, even when we were choked, and morale was low, that nothing could stop us. And nothing had.

Postscript

Our final performance was at Arbeia Roman Fort, South Shields on Tuesday August 31, and again it was sold out. After which the Wall Play and Cloud Nine Troubadours were no more. The company's next production was *Comedy Bites*, the fourth touring show of short comedy sketches we had created to take to pubs, clubs and other small venues. Dave Hollingworth (Loot in *Off the Wall*) was among the cast, but while we were at The Riverdale Hall Hotel, Bellingham for two nights' performances, he took ill. A few days later, on 7 December 2004 he took his own life at his home in Gosforth, Newcastle.

David was a quiet, gentle, private man, of many talents. A respected teacher, and musician as well as an actor, we later learned he was also a gifted writer and had been commissioned to write a play for Hexham Youth Theatre. It was called *Elizabeth's Will*, set in the time of Elizabeth 1st. Several of the company went to see it at The Queens Hall, Hexham. It was a very funny, vividly written piece of work, and we were astounded Dave had never mentioned it.

I was honoured to be among the speakers at his humanist funeral, and we also organised a fund-raising *Day for Dave* back at the Twice Brewed Inn some months later. More than two dozen people walked the play's journey from Gilsland to Twice Brewed, and in the evening the pub's back room (where we'd performed the play) was crammed full. Story teller Chris Bostock (a friend of

Dave's) spun some yarns, Dave's ceilidh band Dog Leap Stars performed, and we showed the full length video of *Off the Wall* which Steve Chettle had made. At the end of the video Steve had affixed a small silent tribute to Dave which seemed unbearably moving. The day and evening raised more than £1,100 for Dave's favourite third world charity, Action Aid. His sister Sue White and close family scattered his ashes up high on the Roman Wall.

His death was a shock to us all. We'd looked forward to his long association with Cloud Nine as actor and as friend. It was a death that illustrated how little we knew about anyone else, for none of us had much inkling of what Dave was battling against. If there were any consolation, it was that he'd shared with the rest of us that unique journey, the record of which is captured in the pages of this book — a book which is dedicated to the memory of Dave Hollingworth.

Off the Wall: the Play

Characters (in order of appearance)

Modern Day
Drysdale: (A small businessman)
Loot: (A large businessman) :
Cogno: (Loot's adviser):
Dolores: (Loot's wife):
Minister: (Govt. Minister for the North):
Starlet: (An hedonistic young female) :

Roman Britain
Guard/Jailer: (Roman Guard):
Briginus: (Caledonian rebel leader)
Prisoner: (A Caledonian prisoner):
Ulpius Marcellus: (Roman Governor of Britain)
Cingetissa: (Briginus' wife):

Several small parts are played by members of the cast

Location: The play is set both in modern and Roman Britain

Time: 21st and 2nd century AD

(the play can be preceded by actors' entry & music as befits)

ENTER LOOT FOLLOWED BY DRYSDALE)

DRYSDALE: Mr Loot, I implore you

LOOT: Look at him. There's something — well, pathetic about him

DRYSDALE: You are a reasonable businessman, I'm sure of that

LOOT: Kicking a man when he's down — it's rather exhilarating really

DRYSDALE: You can see how disastrous this decision would be for the workforce

LOOT: I once took a big juicy bone off a bull terrier. I swear the stupid mutt had the same expression as this creature

DRYSDALE: We are talking here about 800 jobs, and behind each job, a family

LOOT: He's talking, yap, yap, yap. Me? I'm drinking a lightly chilled Martini

DRYSDALE: 800 people on the scrapheap — just like that

LOOT: A green olive or a black olive? These are the decisions men have to make

DRYSDALE: And virtually no redundancy pay

LOOT: I do believe those new razor blades are little better than a lawn mower only delicate skin. What do you think Drysdale?

DRYSDALE: I think Mr Loot that your intention all along was to buy up my company, then close it down

LOOT: How boring most people are. Even my wife Dolores, who by any natural laws of the universe should worship me

DRYSDALE: I thought I had your word. As a gentleman

Loot: Drysdale. How long can you hold your breath for?

Drysdale: What?

Loot: Thirty seconds? One minute? Let's see

Drysdale: I really don't understand —

Loot: Oh come on, don't be a spoilsport. Breathe in. That's it. And hold it. Long as you can. Good boy. Keep going. Good. Good. Excellent Drysdale. especially for someone in your condition. Try it every day, eh? Lots of oxygen to the blood. Here, have my olive, Well, I mustn't detain you. *(PAUSE)* Still here Drysdale?

Drysdale: There was the small matter of my —

Loot: Small matter?

Drysdale: That is, my own compensation — as managing director

Loot: Of course! Forgive me! Here's your cheque *(HANDS OVER)*

Drysdale: One quarter of a million pounds! I don't know what to say

Loot: When holding a quarter of a million pounds in your hand, my advice is to say nothing

Drysdale: It's a lot of money Mr Loot

Loot: Managing directors deserve a lot of money, Drysdale. Now, should you wish this to go to those poor unfortunate 800 unemployed souls, it will come to around £300 apiece. Just say the word. *(PAUSE)* I see. I assume that the matter is now closed. For good. Off you go then, with your cheque *(EXIT DRYSDALE)* Cogno! *(ENTER COGNO)* Large cheques

	concentrate the mind wonderfully against matters of human conscience, don't you find Cogno? Possibly that's why poets are never millionaires
COGNO:	Do you remember a single line of poetry sir?
LOOT:	I'm proud to say I don't. Not any more. There's no money in poetry?
COGNO:	And no poetry in money, some might say
LOOT:	Don't come the smart-arse. Where is that wife of mine?
COGNO:	I believe she's reading
LOOT:	Reading? Reading what?
COGNO:	A book
LOOT:	A book? A wife's place is by her husband. Not with some piddling book. Why does she treat me like this? It's intolerable!
COGNO:	I have the latest letters from your consultants
LOOT:	Give them here *(STARTS OPENING THEM. FIRST ENVELOPE)* Nicaraguan copper to rise moderately Spiffing *(SECOND)* Australian rail network about to reinvest. Earth-shattering (VIEWS MORE.) Rubbish. Rubbish. I've never seen so much — (STOPS TO READ ONE)
COGNO:	You failed to complete your sentence sir. Is it something serious?
LOOT:	Fetch my wife
COGNO:	As I said sir, she's reading
LOOT:	Fetch my wife, insubordinate one! *(EXIT COGNO LOOT HOLDS UP LETTER. ENTER DOLORES)*

DOLORES: Sending for your wife? You must be ill husband. You'll be kissing me next

LOOT: I would kiss you. If you didn't make it feel like kissing a dead fish

DOLORES: That's the feeling exactly isn't it? Your lips were once as hot as fiery coals

LOOT: I still have the same lips Dolores

DOLORES: Me too

LOOT: What do you know about the Roman Wall?

DOLORES: Come again?

LOOT: The Roman Wall woman! Surely those dreary books teach you something? Give me some information

DOLORES: The Roman Wall, also known as Hadrian's Wall began construction in AD122 on the orders of the Emperor Hadrian. The wall was originally built over eight or ten years across what is reputed to be (though this is disputed in some quarters), the narrowest strip of Northern England, from Bowness in Solway in the West to Wallsend, or Segedunum in the East. In the wall's construction more than 25 million facing stones were used

LOOT: Yes, I get the picture

DOLORES: In truth the Emperor Hadrian was only partly responsible for the wall as we are familiar with it. The Romans later attempted to build another wall further North in Scotland, the less ambitious, and much less successful Antonine Wall. When this was abandoned, and the empire retreated back South, Hadrian's Wall was greatly reinforced by the Emperor Severus, for whom much of the credit should belong.

LOOT: I think that will do, wife

DOLORES: Despite this, it is known in common parlance as Hadrian's Wall, and not Severus's Wall. The wall's original length was 80 Roman miles, though at each extremity now only sparse evidence remains. The central part of the wall, situated in the least populated areas, is still, nearly two thousand years on, very spectacular

LOOT: Put a sock in it, right?

DOLORES: Common belief had it the wall was built as a protection from the heathen hordes to the north. Some historians and academics dispute this, claiming the wall was as much an offensive as a defensive weapon

LOOT: You're driving me mad woman! *(TRIES TO STOP HER. SHE PERSISTS IN THE STRUGGLE).*

DOLORES: — and was used by the Romans to launch many raids into the North. During Roman times there was only one written reference which affords us any clue

LOOT: Damn you!

DOLORES: This was the writer Spartianus, who penned Hadrian's biography, including the following: "having restored the army's morale, he (Hadrian) crossed to Britain where he set many things to rights and built a wall 80 miles long to separate the Romans from the barbarians". *(COGNO ENTERS. HAS TO SEPARATE THE TWO OF THEM FROM FIGHTING)*

LOOT: All I ask is some respect!

DOLORES: Respect?

LOOT: I give you everything. You spit in my face

DOLORES: Where is the man I married? The real man?

LOOT: The little man. The man of no consequence

COGNO: Let me clean you up a bit sir *(STARTS)*

LOOT: Clean her up! Make her see sense!

DOLORES: Was there anything else?

LOOT: There was something else Dolores, yes. Who owns the Roman Wall, now?

DOLORES: What is all this about the Roman Wall?

LOOT: I repeat, who owns the wall now?

DOLORES: Very well, various farmers, and landowners. It is under the protection of English Heritage and is managed on behalf of the people

LOOT: Ah, the people. Does it make money?

DOLORES: Thousands flock to see it every year of course, but —

LOOT: *(TO AUDIENCE)* Is that what I asked her Whether thousands flocked to see it every year? Well? Course not. I asked her what — yes, that's right. Does it make money? Maybe Cogno knows the answer to this simple question

COGNO: Income generation is not the Roman Wall's forte, as far as I know sir

LOOT: So. By most definitions, the wall is a failure. I want to buy it

COGNO: Buy it sir?

DOLORES: Did you say — buy it?

LOOT: No, I said there's a walrus eating the inside of my bottom. Yes, buy it, damn you!

COGNO: You want to buy the Roman Wall?

LOOT: I'm in the nation of the deaf, the land of the failed hearing aid. I am among people whose ears contain more wax than a 20ft long candle. Yes — buy it!!

COGNO: But why would you want to buy the Roman Wall?

LOOT: Why?

DOLORES: You hate old things. You hate anything that has a history

LOOT: History is irrelevant

DOLORES: So why buy the wall?

LOOT: Why? Why? Why? Because — because.... *(PAUSE)* I'll tell you why because. Then you'll see. Imagine this. An 80 mile long —

DOLORES: That's Roman miles by the way. By our measurements it is only 73 miles

LOOT: I repeat, an 80 Roman mile long theme park. Customers get to travel the entire original length of the Roman Wall via mono-rail which is sealed in a transparent, weather-proof plastic tunnel

COGNO: Inspired thinking sir

LOOT: There are video screens, holograms, actors dressed as Roman soldiers and barbarians.

COGNO: I see it even as you speak!

LOOT: There are mock battles — an entire full day's travel and adventure without the need to leave your seat.

COGNO: Perfection almost

LOOT: I picture it now! Lionel Loot's Roman Wall Experience. Well?

DOLORES: It stinks

LOOT: What?

DOLORES: Worse than a rotting ferret

LOOT: You devil

DOLORES: Why not walk the wall instead of buying it?

LOOT: Walk the wall?

DOLORES: I might even come with you. Remember, you once walked six miles. Just to bring me an orange

LOOT: That orange was a long time ago. A time of deep foolishness.

DOLORES: I can still taste it

LOOT: It has gone sour. And I suggest you get out *(SHE DOESN'T)* What have I done to deserve this?

COGNO: One question sir on this innovative scheme of yours. Will the farmers sell the land?

LOOT: Farmers are on hard times. Crying into their Range Rovers. Foot and mouth, C.A.P, Set-A-Side. Can't wait to sell up, most of them. So here's some easy loot. From Loot.

COGNO: What about possible government resistance?

LOOT: The government want ventures that produce income How, why, where, and by who are minor considerations. When I tell them what income the Roman Wall Experience will bring in well, game set and match to Loot. Did she say walking? For what? To see a few stones? Grass? Sky? Mud? To be butted by imbecile sheep? Rogered by rampant bulls? Cogno, I want a Feasibility Study done on that wall without delay. And I want its conclusions to mirror my own way of thinking. Oh, and Cogno?

COGNO: Yes sir?

LOOT: I would like it sung

COGNO: I understand *(PAUSE)*

LOOT: Is it done?

COGNO: Naturally *(ENTER SINGER)*

SINGER: *A FEASIBILITY STUDY ON THE ROMAN WALL*

It's only an old wall
80 miles of ancient stone
Grass rocks and sheep that's all
Can't get a signal for the 'phone
You can't eat it ride it play it or invest it
Listen to it, make love to it or text it
It doesn't walk it doesn't dance, it doesn't sing
It doesn't do much of anything

CHORUS: It's only an old wall

DOLORES: Not only an old wall!

LOOT: I've heard worse. Keep going

SINGER: Dead Roman emperors — tell me what is so fantastic?
it needs reinventing with a retail outlet to flash the plastic
Where's the PS2 game, where's the happy meal?
Where's the TV spin-off, just what's the deal?
And why isn't it more like Alton Towers?
There's nothing you can do here

	except walk about for hours and hours and hours?
	Is it cost-effective? I want to know the rate of your return.
	In the end of the day, how much will the damned thing earn?
	It's only an old wall
CHORUS:	It's only an old wall!
LOOT:	Not bad Cogno. Award yourself a bonus.
COGNO:	I already have sir
LOOT:	Now halve it. Dismiss the singer *(COGNO DOES SO)*. I am resolved. I will buy the wall. Impressed Dolores?
DOLORES:	Mountains impress me. Storm clouds. Wind in the trees. A proper lover. A much travelled orange
LOOT:	I once swept you off your feet. I made you breathless
DOLORES:	Yes, you did
LOOT:	I am twice the man I was. Why can't you see that?
DOLORES:	More is often less
LOOT:	That's the kind of idiotic thing your books tell you
DOLORES:	You think you can buy everything. Me, the Roman Wall
LOOT:	Let me educate you my dear. Bring that singer back! *(ENTER SINGER)* Do you know the For Sale song?
SINGER:	It is said to be your anthem Mr Loot
LOOT:	And why not? Sing it for my dear wife

SINGER: Everything is for sale
There's nothing can't be bought
Not just cakes and ale
Not just bread or port
Everything's for sale
You just need to know
The sum that will persuade
The seller to let go

LOOT: Simple really isn't it?

CHORUS: People loyalties land
And the air we breathe
All for sale, you understand
Find the price, then do the deed

LOOT: There's not much more to say

SINGER: Everything is for sale
Just a matter of purchase
The thing that can't be bought
Is the thing that's worthless

DOLORES: Purchase and worthless? You once wrote much better rhymes

LOOT: Me?

DOLORES: Yes, you Loot.

LOOT: Do you have any idea how many factories I own world-wide?

DOLORES: Happily, I'm clueless

LOOT: Not to mention shipping lines

DOLORES: But you have mentioned them

LOOT: I have newspapers in four continents

DOLORES: Why?

LOOT: I own tobacco firms

DOLORES: Smoking improves your wealth?

LOOT: Electricity companies

DOLORES: How shocking

LOOT: Insurance companies, drug companies, construction works —

COGNO: If I might suggest sir, this line of reasoning doesn't appear —

LOOT: Doesn't appear? It appears you are getting beyond yourself Cogno, in matters to do with me and my beloved wife. It appears I deserve an apology

COGNO: My apologies sir

DOLORES: I have some useless books to read *(EXIT DOL)*

LOOT: *(TO COGNO)* I will show her Cogno. Be sure of that. Anyway, do you think I give a toss if she doesn't respect me?

COGNO: As you say sir. And you have bigger fish to fry

LOOT: A very long fish. A fish that you can see from the moon. A brilliant, imaginary, visionary fish Cogno. Another manifestation of my unique skills and talents, skills and talents which my wife singularly fail to acknowledge

COGNO: Not that you give a toss about that of course sir

LOOT: Now listen to me Cogno, we need the government on our side. A £1m donation is to be made to party funds. Donate it via one of our less obviously connected organisations

COGNO: Might I suggest Melrose International Textiles? *(OR INSERT HERE SOME INVENTED NAME TO DO WITH THE VENUE'S LOCALITY)*

Loot: You may. I want the party to be fully aware of the source of the donation. Less so the public

Cogno: £1m is not an inconsiderable amount

Loot: It is only considerable for people who themselves are inconsiderable. All wall landowners are to be wined & dined and made unrefusable offers; shall we say at twice the expected price? There will be conditions re: our use of the wall of course. We shall agree to them. For the moment

Cogno: And when that moment is passed?

Loot: What do you mean?

Cogno: Nothing.

Loot: This Roman Wall. Was it much respected, acclaimed?

Cogno: One of the country's most valued historic monuments

Loot: That's what this country likes, isn't it? Historic monuments. The old, the clapped out, the ruined piles of rubble. Pay the £1m. Let us see the politicians!

(SCENE IS HOUSE OF COMMONS. ENTER MINISTER

Minister: As minister with special responsibility for the North I have been looking at ways of bringing increasing prosperity to this often impoverished region. I have been studying statistics on the North's tourist attractions. Some, such as Tyneside's Metro Centre are highly income generating, others, such as the Roman Wall, though it does attract thousands of visitors annually, less so. Thus Hadrian's Wall makes only a minimal contribution to the

	region's economy. You could say visitors came, they saw, but they did not spend. Thus our govt is moved to look at a radical new departure for the future of the wall, which spans the country from Bowness to Wallsend
MP:	Where?
MINISTER:	To enlighten the Hon. member for Virginia Waters, Bowness is in the county of Cumbria, in the North-West of England, Wallsend is in the conurbation of Tyneside, which is in the North-East *(STILL CONFUSION)* Just think of it as left and right, and up there. *(STARLET ENTERS SAME SIDE AS LOOT)*
STARLET:	You're so clever Mr Loot. Owning all those things
LOOT:	You recognise my genius then?
STARLET:	Such a clever clever boy. Did you mention a present?
LOOT:	I may have
STARLET:	You did. I know you did. You're not like all the rest Mr Loot
LOOT:	That's right. I'm not like all the rest *(GIVES HER A DIAMOND NECKLACE.)*
STARLET:	Have you always been rich, Mr Loot?
LOOT:	For as long as it matters. Though I began with nothing. I crawled up over the vast seething mass of humanity, who were content to wallow in the pit of the mediocre
STAR:	I could fall in love with you Mr Loot
LOOT:	Most women could. But not all. What did I promise you?

STAR 2: You promised me, Mr Loot a brand new coat

LOOT: And I am a man of my word *(HANDS OVER COAT)*.

STARLET: I've been dreaming of you Mr Loot

LOOT: You have?

STAR: And I've been dreaming of that expensive perfume you said you'd buy me

LOOT: My wife won't wear it

STAR 3: I'll wear it

LOOT: Do you think it's obscenely expensive?

STAR 3: Oh yes! *(HE GIVES HER PERFUME. SHE SPRAYS IT ON AND EXITS. LOOT CONTINUES TO OBSERVE THE MINISTER)*

MINISTER:: Our objective is to bring in the vigour of private capital in order that the Roman Wall may realise its full commercial potential, while we retain some measure of public control. We have drawn up proposals with the various landowners and invited one of our most respected entrepreneurs, Lionel Loot, to create an entirely new concept, both educational and recreational, and of course grounded in the wall's unique history *(OPPOSITION MP INTERRUPTS)*

OPP MP: Might I ask the Minister, is the plan actually to sell the Roman Wall to Lionel Loot?

MINISTER:: Within certain restrictions, yes. Mr Loot hopes to create along the wall length, an exciting and dynamic new opportunity *(GOV MP INTERRUPTS)*

GOV MP: Would the minister inform us if this exciting

	new project will create new jobs in a region traditionally short of employment?
MINISTER:	Statistics forecast 500 new jobs along the Wall's length, annual visitors rising to 5m within three years, and injection into the local economy of £120m *(OPP. MP. INTERRUPTS)*
OPP MP:	Mr Speaker, In my opinion these proposals will drastically alter the character of this unique monument, turning it into little more than a glorified Disneyland
MINISTER:	The member opposite is trapped both by the past and by prejudice. If our country is to be at the forefront of global development, we cannot afford to stay still *(LOOT IS STILL WATCHING. ENTER DOLORES)*
DOLORES:	What is that smell?
LOOT:	Smell?
DOLORES:	Perfume. And not mine
LOOT:	What are you suggesting?
DOLORES:	*(SINGS)* It's not Chanel or Givenchy And you can't convince me That it's *L'Air du Temps* Or even Yardley In fact I can hardly Tell what it is at all *(END OF SONG)* Am I being a fool, Loot?
LOOT:	You are my wife, Mother of our two sons. You have everything you need.
DOLORES:	We both have then. Everything we need
LOOT:	Exactly *(EXIT DOLORES, WE RETURN TO THE CHAMBER)*

SPEAKER:	We move to the vote. All those in favour of the Roman Wall Experience Bill. *(SOUNDS OFF OF "AYE!")*. All those against? *(LESS NOISE FOR "NO!")* The ayes to the right have it. The ayes to the right have it. *(EXIT MPS ET AL. ENTER COGNO)*
LOOT:	I give them what they want Cogno, even before they know they want it. That is why I am me, and they are they. Let the construction of the Roman Wall Experience begin! Build the perspex weather proof tunnel! *(ALL THE FOLLOWING ARE ANIMATED)*
LOOT:	Assemble and secure the 80 mile long monorail system! Install the one dozen giant touch button information screens! Activate the Roman centurion holograms! Complete conversion of 12 mile castles to pizza and burger bars! Choreograph and synchronise the warring Picts and Scots armies! The small details Cogno, I leave to you. Have I missed anything?
COGNO:	I believe the Lionel Loot Roman Wall Experience awaits the official opening
LOOT:	The guest list?
COGNO:	All in order. The PM will be there, Elton John, Charlie Boy, Posh and Becks, Jonathan Ross. The latest Big Brother winner
LOOT:	Is the hospitality tent stocked with the finest smoked salmon and strawberries?
COGNO:	It is
LOOT:	The champagne?

COGNO:	The Moet is ready to pop
LOOT:	Hot air balloons?
COGNO:	122 of them, to mark the year that construction of the wall began, will rise at the given signal along the length of the wall
LOOT:	The Red Arrows?
COGNO:	Flying in a direct line from Segedunum to Bowness, leaving a vapour trail of purple. The colour of Imperial Rome
LOOT:	The Italian ambassador?
COGNO:	Already in the hospitality tent and slightly drunk
LOOT:	Where is Dolores?
COGNO:	Resting sir
LOOT:	Resting — for my moment of glory? She deliberately taunts me. I want my wife here. Now
COGNO:	Very well *(EXITS. LOOT GREETS VARIOUS INVISIBLE GUESTS. ENTER DOLORES. DRUNK)* How nice of you to put in an appearance
DOLORES:	All this has nothing to do with me Loot
COGNO:	Of course not. I did it. Nevertheless, smile for the Environment Minister. Are you not impressed?
DOLORES:	Impressed?
COGNO:	Look at them. They're all impressed. And I'm not even married to them
DOLORES:	*(SINGS)* They're sycophants, they're hangers-on

> Free-loaders each and every one
> They'll scoff your food, they'll down your liquor
> A rotting rat couldn't make me sicker
> They sniff round fame, money and power
> I'd boot them out, the whole bloody shower

COGNO: Ah — Secretary of State! Charmed you could make it! *(TO DOLORES)*. What do I need to do for you? Do you realise just how many women with lives of poverty and misery would die to be in your shoes right now?

DOLORES: You know nothing about such women. And they can have my shoes! *(REMOVES SHOES)*

LOOT: Dolores. The PM is watching. Please replace those shoes

DOLORES: That's what you care about. That your rich and influential friends might see your wife without her shoes. The utter total shame of it. Look, the shoeless wife of Lionel Loot!

LOOT: Am I to be humiliated at my moment of triumph? By my own wife?

DOLORES: *(SHOUTS)* I hope you all drop dead! *(THEY GRAPPLE. ENTER COGNO TO SEPARATE THEM)*

COGNO: Sir, the official opening ceremony

LOOT: Of course *(STEPS UP)* Friends, honoured guests. How delighted I am you could attend this historic occasion that both celebrates the past, acknowledges the present and anticipates the future. The Lionel Loot Roman Wall Experience bridges the culture gap, allowing the public to enjoy this historic monument in a unique way.

DOLORES: Bollocks!

LOOT: In one moment I will ask the honoured guests to step into the mono-rail cars. This is a photo-opportunity, so members of press and media please be ready. In closing I would just like to say that in modern Britain it is the energy drive and vision of private enterprise that propels these projects forward.

DOLORES: Loot — where have you gone?

LOOT: I am delighted that this government recognises the need to encourage that same energy, drive and vision. Thank you. *(STEPS DOWN, SHAKES VARIOUS INVISIBLE HANDS ETC. DOLORES IS ON THE SIDELINES, HE TALKS ACROSS TO HER AS HE SHAKES HANDS ETC).* You see? I am valued, and respected. But not by you, Never by you. *(EXIT DOLORES. ENTER STARLET)*

STARLET: You're a real man Mr Loot

LOOT: I know one who doesn't think so

STARLET: How does it feel, to be a man like you?

LOOT: Why not you, Dolores?

STARLET: And all this is yours?

LOOT: What?

STARLET: All this is yours

LOOT: Yes, mine. Everything I see. Everything I touch *(LOOKS HER UP AND DOWN)* is mine

STARLET: And you can do whatever you like with it?

LOOT: Who could stop me?

STARLET: Gee! I've never met a man like you Mr Loot

LOOT: That's right. You've never met a man like me
(EXIT STARLET. ENTER COGNO)

LOOT: You have the first six months report, Cogno?

COGNO: Safely stored in my head sir

LOOT: Tell me

COGNO: The first six months of the Lionel Loot Roman Wall Experience have been a runaway commercial success

LOOT: As I knew they would be

COGNO: Tickets and commodity sales are 15 per cent higher than projections, and the profitability rate is 22 per cent

LOOT: They'll buy anything Cogno. I despise them all. Little people. 22 per cent? The kind of figure I like. Do you know what women admire in men?

COGNO: It is a secret alas, to which I am not privy sir

LOOT: Of course not. It's the brilliance of success that dazzles women Cogno. How fortunate not everyone can be successful

COGNO: Some of us are born merely to serve sir

LOOT: I never know when you're taking the piss

COGNO: Surely by now sir...

LOOT: She was my heartbeat Cogno. The blood that flowed in my veins. I can have any woman I please

COGNO: Of course. You asked for an audience with the Minister. The Minister is here

LOOT: Is he a reptile? A slug? Something found under a rock?

COGNO: I believe his name is Jeremy

LOOT: An underling. Let him slither in *(EXIT COGNO. TO AUDIENCE.)* What do I care for such grey functionaries, persons with the imaginations of potato peel, *(COGNO — ENTERS WITH MINISTER. EXIT COGNO)*

MINISTER: Mr Loot. Delighted. The government is exceedingly pleased with the figures thus far for the Roman Wall Experience.

LOOT: I think you'll find the correct title is The Lionel Loot Roman Wall Experience.

MINISTER: Of course

LOOT: Say it then!

MINISTER: The government is exceedingly pleased with The Lionel Loot Roman Wall Experience.

LOOT: I'm sure Especially as the theme park passes through two marginal constituencies

MINISTER: All factors are relevant. At the end of the day, given a level playing field, we have rebuffed critics claiming we neglect the rural Northern economy. The Wall's success enables us to ring-fence certain priorities, and assures a customer satisfaction level commensurate with expectations

LOOT: Customer?

MINISTER: Yes, customer

LOOT: You mean, the voters?

MINISTER: The party has found the use of consumerist terminology is in tune with market trends. You requested an audience Mr Loot?

LOOT: In non-consumerist terminology, I would now like this government to remove all the restrictions as to how I make use of the wall and surrounding land

MINISTER: Lift all restrictions?

LOOT: At least your hearing is — what? — commensurate with expectations

MINISTER: But I don't understand

LOOT: Life is so complex, I agree. But listen, it's simple enough. The wall is now mine. I should be allowed to do what I like with it

MINISTER: We are talking here about an important historic monument

LOOT: And I have made this historic monument highly lucrative.

MINISTER: Agreed

LOOT: And can make it even more so

MINISTER: More so? Perhaps you could elucidate

LOOT: Perhaps I could. Lift the restrictions and I guarantee, the financial benefit to the government will be many many times what it is now. Your customers will be delighted. You could even cut taxes

MINISTER: Cut taxes?

LOOT: Quite a shock isn't it? Tax cuts for the better-off, of course

MINISTER: I see

LOOT: Imagine. The PM need never again face the nightmare prospect of taxing the rich more than the poor

MINISTER: Give me the main bullet points of your proposal

LOOT: Bullet points?

MINISTER: Points one, two, three etc

LOOT: Tax cuts, tax cuts, and tax cuts

MINISTER: The Wall has always had special protection. What you are asking is highly unusual

LOOT: Imagine the beneficial headlines in the Daily Mail. The praise from The Sun. I am talking the greatest tax cuts in living memory

MINISTER: But to lift all restrictions on the Roman Wall

LOOT: What do restrictions do — except restrict?

MINISTER: Yes. I see

LOOT: Restricted use of old stones, or £20 a month more in take-home pay

MINISTER: £20 a month?

LOOT: Like I say, tax cuts, tax cuts, and tax cuts

MINISTER: Why not simply tell me these — expansion plans?

LOOT: I am a businessman. Businessmen reveal their full plans only at the most opportune moment.

MINISTER: I can assure you of this government's full confidentiality

LOOT: I've seen their full confidentiality on the front of the tabloids. Well? I'm a busy man

MINISTER: I shall see what I can do

LOOT: Good boy. Report well to your master. And be quick about it. Have a pleasant journey
(ENTER COGNO AND LEADS MINISTER

OFF). Exit one fool. Enter one very important lady. And who in this decaying country deserves it more than Lionel Loot? Eh, Cogno? *(ENTER THE QUEEN WITH CEREMONIAL SWORD)*

Queen: Well?

Loot: I'm ready *(KNEELS ETC IN PREPARATION)*

Queen: One is disinclined *(EXIT QUEEN)*

Loot: Bugger

Cogno: She's smaller than I imagined

Loot: You think it's funny?

Cogno: Moderately

Loot: Maybe you'll find this funny? *(PRODUCES LETTER)*

Cogno: I was wondering when that would put in another appearance

Loot: Have you the remotest idea what it contains?

Cogno: Would that I did, sir

Loot: And my wife, do you think she has the remotest ideas what's in it? *(ENTER DOLORES)*

Dolores: And how could I?

Loot: How could you? Of course. Who needs the Queen? Who needs the rest of the cretins? What was the one really important group I couldn't join? The high power global club that controls the world's economy? The place where a man such as I should belong. But it's a bit exclusive you might say... Until now. Now they can't keep me out.

Cogno: They, sir?

DOLORES: You're talking in riddles

LOOT: Let me spell it out then. To both of you. O-I-L

COGNO: O-I-L?

DOLORES: Oil?

DOLORES: And what about it?

LOOT: What about it? What about it? *(HANDS LETTER OVER)* That's what about it *(THEY BOTH READ IT)*

DOLORES: So this was your plan all along?

LOOT: Of course it was!

COGNO: And the Lionel Loot Roman Wall Experience?

LOOT: A trashy means to an end.

COGNO: So your actual interest in the Roman Wall is minimal?

LOOT: Lumps of old stone? What on earth do I want with lumps of old stone. Unless of course —

DOLORES: Beneath that old stone is oil

LOOT: Billions and billions of barrels of premium grade oil. *(TAKES LETTER)* Vital and exclusive information from my contact. A top man in the geological field

COGNO: So you were just softening up the government for the real prize?

LOOT: The Prix d'Honneur, The Blue Ribbon, the gold medal you might say.

DOLORES: And how many miles of the Roman Wall do you intend to demolish to gain access to these oil supplies?

LOOT: Oh, not more than 12 or 15. The Steel Rigg area.

COGNO: The wall's most spectacular stretch

LOOT: Let the wall earn real money Cogno. It was built for a purpose, not just for gawping at. Let's give it back a purpose. What can old stones earn? Look at this *(PRODUCES LOOT OIL SIGN)*. My product will run through the arteries of the entire planet. Every day millions of thirsty vehicles seeking out this sign

COGNO: And what of public reactions to your Roman Wall demolition plans?

LOOT: There will be some voices in opposition. The balance sheet will win the day. It always does. My finest moment. I am basking in my triumph. Nothing can stand in my way. Be proud to be called Lionel Loot's wife

DOLORES: All this for oil Lionel?

LOOT: What?

DOLORES: For oil?

LOOT: Yes oil! Oil that fuels the world economy. Oil keeps that keeps things moving, oil that keeps you warm. Oil that... oh, tell her Cogno!

COGNO: Your husband Madame was hoping this piece of entrepreneurial skill might endear you to him *(DOL LAUGHS)*

LOOT: What the hell is she laughing at?

COGNO: Part laughter sir. Part tears

LOOT: Now listen to me. All these years I have fought my way up. I have battled against dysfunctional governments, crooks, idiots, plum-faced buffoons in old school ties, civil servants who have been brain-dead for years, clapped out institutions and regulations, the whole turgid treacle you wade through to make good in this country. And now finally I have broken through, I have achieved what no single individual ever achieved, and what is the reaction of my wife? All this is for oil?

DOLORES: Well?

LOOT: *(SONG)* I'll suck it from the earth
I'll pump it near and far
That silent hidden lake
Black blood of motor car

DOLORES: You've got luxury homes on four continents
Accountants agree your finances make a lot of sense
You've got servants to cut off your bacon rind
But if you look deep then you'll find
No respect

LOOT: Though half the world is starving
Motors' bellies must be filled
Gurgling from the pumps
With a heartbeat never stilled

LOOT: Oil is my black blood
Oil will cleanse my soul
Oil will spread its stain
Oil will make me whole

DOLORES: You've got companies in textiles chemicals and computer ware
Theme parks, insurance, even Loot Air
Stock markets tremble when your shares fluctuate
But what you ain't got, you'll find too late
My respect

LOOT:	Every time they press the pedal Every time they turn the key Oil runs through their engines Oil is me
DOLORES:	In the Rich List you make the Top Ten Five billion you earn, then five billion again But someday in the back of your Bentley A voice will whisper gently No respect
LOOT:	Oil is my black blood Oil will cleanse my soul Oil will spread its stain Oil will make me whole
LOOT:	I cannot speak to her Cogno. Damn her to hell!
DOLORES:	And damn him to hell as well Cogno. Got that have you?
COGNO:	I believe I have, yes
LOOT:	Fetch me a real woman, Cogno
COGNO:	What?
LOOT:	Someone who admires and respects me.
COGNO:	I'm not sure that is a good idea sir, I —
LOOT:	I don't give a parrot's toenail what you're sure about. Just do it!
DOLORES:	Yes Cogno! Give him one of his floozies,
COGNO:	Madame, I think —
LOOT:	Do it!
DOLORES:	Do it!
COGNO:	This is bad business *(COGNO EXITS.RETURNS WITH STARLET)*
STAR:	Lionel!

LOOT:	Say you respect me
STARLET:	Course I respect you. Anything you like
LOOT:	Show me you respect me *(SHE KISSES HIM)*
LOOT:	My wife doesn't respect me
STAR:	Wives don't know everything *(THEY KISS AGAIN)*
COGNO:	Come away Madame *(SHE WON'T)* End it sir, now *(HE WON'T)* Then let it pursue its own fate *(LOOT GETS AMOROUS WITH STARLET IN FRONT OF DOLORES)*
LOOT:	All your fault Dolores. All your fault
DOLORES:	Be it on your own head *(LOOT GOES THROUGH A TRANSFORMATION . EMERGES ON THE FLOOR OF A ROMAN PRISON AT VINDOL ANDA, A FORT NEAR THE ROMAN WALL IN ANCIENT BRITAIN. ANOTHER MALE PRISONER IS SHAKING HIM)*
PRISONER:	Briginus — wake up!
LOOT:	What?
PRISONER:	The jailer will be here for you soon Briginus
LOOT:	What?
PRISONER:	You mustn't weaken, leader *(ENTER JAILER)*
JAILER:	Alright you snivelling pieces of dung, you fetid waste products
PRISONER:	You can't talk to him like that
JAILER:	Oh begging your pardon, I'm sure, you steaming cow pat
PRISONER:	Have you any idea who he is?

JAILER:	Let me think now. He's a turd, he's an insect. he's a piece of Caledonian puke, who along with several others, including you, breached one of our mile castles and is soon to be nailed up on a crucifix where he'll very slowly, and very agonisingly die. Same as you. Now, did I miss anything?
PRISONER:	He is Briginus, Caledonian Chieftain
JAILER:	Yeah, and I'm the Emperor of Rome
PRISONER:	See for yourself. Show him Briginus!
LOOT:	Show him what?
PRISONER:	Show him the tattoo! *(REVEALS A TATTOO ON LOOT)*
JAILER:	Let me see that. *(CHECKS)* Blimey!
LOOT:	What the —?
PRISONER:	I suggest you treat him with some respect
LOOT:	A tattoo?
JAILER:	What's a Caledonian chieftain doing, vandalising one of our mile castles?
PRISONER:	Like all true Caledonians, whatever rank, he wants the Romans out of Britain
LOOT:	Now listen —
JAILER:	The prat. Hasn't he heard? Most of the chieftains enjoy Roman hospitality, women, banquets, wine. I've seen them at it, hobnobbing with the governor. Nice work if you can get it, eh?
PRISONER:	Briginus is not like the others
LOOT:	What the hell are you two talking about?

JAILER: You're honoured, mate. Ulpius Marcellus is right here at Vindolanda

PRISONER: How about that Briginus! The Roman Governor of Britain. Polluting our Northern air

JAILER: Ambitious bloke Ulpius. Plans to go far. And he's well and truly choked. Some of you heathens murdered a Roman general. Now you're breaking through the wall. Rome doesn't like it. It's got to stop. And he's the man sent by Rome to stop it. Nothing like a few crucifixions to quieten the mob

LOOT: Who the devil are you people?

PRISONER: Briginus, demand to see this Ulpius Marcellus. Tell him resistance will never cease, until the last Roman has left Britain.

JAILER: Oh, I'm sure the governor will see him. Now he knows who he is. These fat cats stick together in my experience. Probably get off scot-free, your great chieftain. Unlike you, poor sod. Ever seen a crucifixion? If it wasn't for the pain of the nails through your wrists your arms would ache something terrible. Course, you might get strangulation. Eyes-a-popping and all that

PRISONER: Do you think for one minute Briginus would collude with the Roman empire? His heart is with his people.

JAILER: Course it is, sunshine.

LOOT: Now listen you two, put an end to this nonsense now, and I'll ensure leniency. Continue, and it will go very very bad for you. This I guarantee

JAILER:	You wait here, chieftain or no chieftain. I'll get word to our governor just who he's got locked up, He'll be very interested I'm sure. Now don't go away, there's good boys *(EXIT JAILER)*
PRISONER:	He will try to buy you off Briginus. He doesn't realise who he's dealing with
LOOT:	Have you heard nothing I've said?
PRISONER:	The Romans rule by terror. But also persuasion, He will offer you the good life. For your subservience. And our slavery. The Romans believe everyone is for sale
LOOT:	You are clearly suffering total delusion
PRISONER:	If you give a lead, your people will follow *(ENTER JAILER)*
JAILER:	You, Chieftain, follow me. The governor wants to see you. And you? You can rot a bit longer
PRISONER:	What about some food?
JAILER:	Just eaten thank you. Nice leg of rabbit *(EXIT PRISONER WITH BRIGINUS. TO MEET WITH ULPIUS MAXIMUS. THE TWO SPEAK IN LATIN. ENGLISH IN ITALICS)* *Adest, legate* (he is here Governor)
ULPIUS:	*Quis adeste?* (Who is here?)
JAILER:	*Briginus* (Briginus)
ULPIUS:	*Quis vero Briginus?* (And who exactly is Briginus?)
JAILER:	*Duc Caledonius, qui nuper per vallum irrupit* (The Caledonian chieftain, who recently breached the wall)
ULPIUS:	*Esto; veniat* (let's see him then)

LOOT: But you're talking gibberish

JAILER: Are you insulting the language of Imperial Rome?

LOOT: What?

JAILER: You don't think we'd converse in all this Celtic crap? *(BRINGS LOOT FORWARD. ULPIUS DISMISSES JAILER)*

ULPIUS: You've been a naughty boy, chieftain or no chieftain

LOOT: Do you have any idea who I am?

ULPIUS: Of course. Naughty boy. Now, I have been known to forgive naughty boys. Have some wine. Bulgaria's finest. Causing criminal damage? A chieftain? Oh dear.

LOOT: My name is Lionel Loot. I am among the richest men in Britain. I am about to become an oil magnate.

ULPIUS: Let's face it, Hadrian's Wall. A fiasco. It takes 20,000 troops to man the damned thing. Out of 50,000 for these entire islands. If it was left to me dear boy, I'd up sticks and leave the heathens to their own business — no offence of course. Strictly entre nous, what is Rome doing in this godforsaken hole? There is a limit, especially a northern limit. A long way from Rome, you might say. Placate the north Ulpius, that's what they said. Placate the north? You might as well try to placate a hurricane. Can't just keep pouring in more troops. The senate's getting restless. Anyway, I do understand the Caledonian frustrations dear boy. I mean, you were born in the damned place. But vandalising the wall — A chieftain? Not really on now, is it?

Loot: My patience is about exhausted

Ulpius: They respect you Briginus. If you tell them it is in their best interests to end this resistance, they will end it. And you of course will be a free man. And a good ally to Rome. Rome looks after its allies. The others must die of course

Loot: Others?

Ulpius: Your fellow terrorists. Rome has to set an example. But you Briginus —

Loot: Now listen one last time. I am Lionel Loot, entrepreneur, businessman. Whoever this damned fellow is, it is not me. I am not Briginus

Ulpius: What?

Loot: You have no idea little man. The Loot empire is global. Whoever you are, I could have you swotted away like a fly

Ulpius: You say you are not Briginus? Is this some kind of game?

Loot: Lionel Loot does not play games.

Ulpius: Guard *(ENTER GUARD)* Beat him *(GUARD DOES SO)* Well? Speak, fool

Loot: What, I —

Ulpius: Beat him again. *(DOES SO).* Now crucify him. With the rest of them. Do it now! *(GUARD STARTS TAKING LOOT OFF)* Leave him 48 hours on the cross. Let him suffer

Loot: Wait!

Ulpius: No mercy to impostors. Get him out!

Loot: No, wait — the tattoo! *(SHOWS IT)*. See! *(ULPIUS CHECKS)* Proof! I am Briginus! Spare me!

Ulpius: What kind of fool game are you playing with the Governor of Britain?

Loot: No, no game. no, I swear. A misunderstanding

Ulpius: Bring him here guard *(IS DRAGGED THERE)* You swear on the life of all you hold dear; you are Briginus, Caledonian chieftain?

Loot: I swear. I am Briginus

Ulpius: The Romans show no mercy to fool or tricksters

Loot: But I have the tattoo. That proves I am Briginus!

Ulpius: What did the terrorists call him in the cells, Guard?

Guard: Oh, they called him Briginus alright. Quite the favourite he was! They looked up to the little turd. A sort of saviour

Ulpius: We shall see. Now listen. A document will be drawn stating that you accept Roman rule unconditionally, and urge all other Caledonians to do likewise. You will make your sign on this acceptance which will then be made public in your presence

Loot: And if I agree, I go free?

Ulpius: Yes

Loot: I'll sign it

Ulpius: Of course, acceptance would confer certain personal privileges on yourself and —

Loot: I said I'll sign the damned thing

ULPIUS: And though you may on one level see it as betraying your countrymen, on another — what did you say?

LOOT: I said I'll sign it

ULPIUS: You, Briginus, rebel chieftain of the Caledonians, will readily agree to sign this document?

LOOT: Didn't I just say so?

ULPIUS: To accept the power and superiority of Rome, its legal right to rule over Britain?

LOOT: As long as it gets me out of this damned place

ULPIUS: No torture? No coercion? Emperor Severus will be delighted. Guard, have the document prepared! And I warn you, if this is some kind of trick —

LOOT: Just do it!

ULPIUS: Call a public meeting for tomorrow. An important announcement. Oh, and Briginus?

LOOT: What?

ULPIUS: We have now captured your wife, Cingetissa.

LOOT: My wife?

ULPIUS: You remember your wife of course. A wild one alright. Put up a struggle when we caught her. Our soldiers have got three split heads to prove it. You look surprised

LOOT: No, it's just that I —

ULPIUS: She's not playing ball. But I'm sure you'll talk her round. Make her see sense. Just like you, eh? This story has not finished yet. *(EXIT ULPIUS. PRISONER AND DOLORES ENTER)*

GUARD: Here he is — your great leader

DOLORES: Briginus!

LOOT: Dolores!

PRISONER: Cingetissa

LOOT: Cingetissa?

DOLORES: You are alive! *(EMBRACES HIM)* My noble husband

PRISONER: Briginus — how exactly did you tell that Ulpius Marcellus he could stuff it?

GUARD: *(HITS HIM)* Show some respect to the governor, Caledonian cur!

DOLORES: Your speech to the tribe was magnificent, your bravery and selflessness in leading the wall raid. I am proud of you Briginus. Our two sons are proud of you

GUARD: Just shut it lady, alright? *(MANHANDLES HER. SHE SPITS AT HIM)*. You are not fit to lick my husband's boots

GUARD: *(SLAPS HER)* Caledonian bitch! *(LOOT RESTRAINS HIM)* Here, don't you go and spoil it sunshine. Don't forget whose side you're on, otherwise — *(EXITS AND RETURNS RAPIDLY WITH DOCUMENT)* Seen this, have you?

LOOT: *(LOOKS AT IT)* But that's ridiculous — I can't read this?

GUARD: Since when could any Caledonian read, chieftain or no Chieftain? Ready for this, are you, Mrs Chieftain? *(DOLORES SPITS AT HIM)* Go on then. Have your fun. Now it's my turn. *(READS)* "I Briginus, Chieftain of the Caledonian Tribe do hereby renounce my destructive struggle against Imperial Rome and do urge all my fellow tribes people to do likewise; to cease their terrorist resistance against the Imperial Roman Army and I hereby pledge my undying loyalty to both Ulpius Marcellus, governor of Britain, and to Septimus Severus, Emperor of Rome." This to be pro claimed publicly at Vindolanda at sunrise tomorrow, and Briginus's mark to be attached here *(BOTH DOLORES & PRISONER LAUGH)*

DOLORES: What is this nonsense? Have you any idea the kind of man you're dealing with?

GUARD: More than you, darling

DOLORES: Tell him Briginus

GUARD: Yeah, why don't you just tell me Briginus?

PRISONER: Tell him what it means to lead the Caledonian tribe

DOLORES: To risk everything for what you believe in. To be — a man

GUARD: Your mark right there at the bottom if you will, great leader *(HANDS DOCUMENT TO HIM)*

DOLORES: Tell him how you once rode three days and nights to fetch medicine for a sick elder of the village

PRISONER: Tell him how you didn't sleep for a week searching for a missing child

DOLORES: Or maybe we'll tell him. Do not insult this man with your — document. He would lay down his own life for his tribes people

GUARD: Oh dear. Oh dear, oh dear.

DOLORES: Shall I trample it, or will you Briginus?

PRISONER: Let us both trample it. Together

GUARD: The mark, if you please

LOOT: You don't understand — either of you. I have to sign

GUARD: What's that saying? The thing that can't be bought is the thing that's worthless. Sorry about all this lady. Fat cats do tend to stick together though, whatever side they're on. And Ulpius will also spare you, being a chieftain's wife and all. Course, this one *(INDICATES PRISONER)* is for it. We've already made an example of his eldest son. To encourage the others you might say here's a little keepsake. Your son's right hand. *(HANDS OVER TO PRISONER)* I'll take that document, great leader.

DOLORES: From this day, nothing is true.

PRISONER: My son is dead. Now we are all truly dead. And you, our murderer

DOLORES: The man I loved! The man I respected above all men!

LOOT: But — you don't understand. You don't know who I am

DOLORES: Then who are you?

LOOT: What?

DOLORES: Who are you?

GUARD: The document if you don't mind, great leader

DOLORES: Decide now. Who are you?

GUARD: Let's get on with it.

LOOT:	Who am I?
DOLORES:	A simple question
LOOT:	This document will save both our lives!
DOLORES:	It will condemn us. And our people. Decide who you are
LOOT:	So you just want to die?
DOLORES:	Your last chance. Decide who you are
GUARD:	Enough messing about —
LOOT:	I am —
GUARD:	"I am — I am." You are a thick Caledonian out to save his skin. Your mark!
DOLORES:	Briginus. By all the love I have for you
LOOT:	I am —
PRISONER:	Briginus. You are not like other men-
GUARD:	Just stick your mark on, you ignorant pig. Sign it — pig! *(LOOT EVENTUALLY CASTS DOCUMENT AWAY)*
GUARD:	Oh, very clever. Fine. Now, I wonder what the governor would say about that *(ENTER GOVERNOR)*
ULPIUS:	The governor would say, crucify all three at sunset. High treason against Imperial Rome. At sunset! *(EXIT GOVERNOR)*
LOOT:	What have I done?
DOLORES:	The only thing my husband ever could do
PRISONER:	Our chieftain could act no other way. Hail Briginus!
DOLORES:	Our love can never die Briginus. We face only mortal death. *(THEY KISS. THIS KISS*

TRANSPORTS HIM BACK TO THE 21st CENTURY. LOOT IS WITH THE STARLET RATHER THAN CINGETISSA)

STARLET: You're not like other men Mr Loot

LOOT: What?

STARLET: And like I say, wives don't know everything. Have a bit of fun eh?

LOOT: Get out!

STAR: But what about my present and —

LOOT: Now!

STARLET: Charming, I'm sure *(EXITS. ENTER COGNO)*

COGNO: Sir, the Minister for the North is here

LOOT: What?

COGNO: Some good news I imagine

LOOT: News?

COGNO: Possibly soon you will be a member of the most exclusive club in the industrial world. Loot Oil will be born.

LOOT: Where is Cingetissa?

COGNO: Cingetissa?

LOOT: Dolores — my wife

COGNO: She is about to leave. For good

LOOT: Bring her to me! Now!

COGNO: Yes sir. Meantime, the Minister! *(EXIT COGNO. ENTER MINISTER. SAME ACTOR AS ULPIUS)*

MINISTER: Mr Loot

LOOT: You! Ulpius!

MINISTER: Sir?

LOOT: You wish to placate the North, yes?

MINISTER: Excuse me?

LOOT: You have a document?

MINISTER: Yes. Mr Loot, this document gives you total rights over the wall and adjacent property; rights which we are confident you will develop in line with — *(ENTER DOLORES)*

DOLORES: Well?

LOOT: Dolores!

DOLORES: How long does it take?

LOOT: Take?

DOLORES: For a man to know who he is

MINISTER: Your signature sir?

LOOT: You — him...? How much do you know — either of you?

COGNO: Know sir?

DOLORES: About what?

LOOT: About Ulpius Marcellus, for one

DOLORES: The Roman Governor of Britain brought in to suppress the Caledonians?

LOOT: And what about Septimus Severus?

COGNO: Wasn't he the Roman Emperor at roughly the same period?

DOLORES: I believe so

LOOT: Or Briginus, Caledonian chieftain

COGNO: Well, I'm not sure, I —

LOOT: His wife Cingetissa

DOLORES: Cingetissa? A lovely name

LOOT: Crucified, both of them. For resisting the mighty power of Rome. They died together. As they had lived together

MINISTER: If you wouldn't mind Mr Loot. The signature

COGNO: Sunset soon sir

LOOT: What?

COGNO: I just thought you'd like to know. Sunset soon

DOLORES: Always the saddest time of the day. A time something dies

LOOT: Sunset? Wait! *(LOOKS AT TATTOO)* The tattoo! But that's impossible —

DOLORES: I'm sure you've always had that tattoo Lionel

COGNO: Is it not a part of you sir, that tattoo

MINISTER: If I could just hurry your signature along sir

LOOT: *(TO MINISTER)* Get out!

MINISTER: But sir, the signature and —

LOOT: Are you deaf? *(EXIT MINISTER. LOOT TEARS UP DOCUMENT*

COGNO: The empire crumbles

DOLORES: As all empires must

LOOT: I don't understand

COGNO: Course you do

LOOT: It's over, isn't it?

DOLORES: It's just beginning

LOOT: All that stuff. The journey's over

DOLORES: What journey would you travel for me Lionel?

LOOT: To get what?

DOLORES: A single orange

LOOT: I would journey — the length of the Roman Wall. On foot

DOLORES: Lead on *(THEY KISS. MUSIC, DANCING)*

END OF PLAY

This play was first produced in August 2004, opening on August 19 at Lindow Hall, Bowness-on-Solway, and touring the Roman Wall on foot. The final production was at Arbeia Roman Fort, South Shields, on Tuesday August 31. The cast on this tour were: Dylan Mortimer; Dave Hollingworth; Bill E. Meeks; Janine Birkett; Alex Kinsey; Susie Burton.